DOCUMENTATION MANUAL

AUERBACH Computer Science Series

Ned Chapin, Ph.D., General Editor

NED CHAPIN *Flowcharts*

BARY W. POLLACK, ed. *Compiler Techniques*

COMTRE CORPORATION, Edited by ANTHONY P. SAYERS *Operating Systems Survey*

JOHN K. LENHER *Flowcharting: An Introductory Text and Workbook*

J. VAN DUYN *Documentation Manual*

DOCUMENTATION MANUAL

J. VAN DUYN

philadelphia
new york
london

Published simultaneously in Canada by Book Center, Inc.

Library of Congress Catalog Card Number: 76-189532
International Standard Book Number: 0-87769-117-7

First Printing

Printed in the United States of America

CONTENTS

LIST OF FIGURES

PREFACE

This book was written in response to a very real need in the commercial data processing field for a concise, lucid, painless, and, above all, functional guidebook *with examples* for computer programmers, systems analysts, management, and nonprogramming users.

Accordingly, in this simply defined, easy to follow text, I have included:

Sample documented applications at the end of each section to give an empirical illustration of the text.

Samples of system and program flowcharts, using ANS (American National Standards) standard flow chart symbols.

Samples of innovative cross-index tables such as "Visual Chart of Programs and Files," "File Creation Flow Table," "Report Creation Flow Table," and so on.

Samples of Data File/Report Nomenclature and General EDP Glossary. Such information is very important in any documentation, to clarify the standard EDP terms for nonprogramming personnel as well as the specific terminology unique to each computer facility.

Model formats of "Documentation Acceptance Checklist," "Control Checklist," etc. These checklists are to insure that each system and all programs in that system are being documented and included in that particular section.

I would like to express my appreciation to: Clair Althouse, John Sullivan, Peter Dolan, Fred Brand, Judy Golub, Steve Lubeck, and Lockheed Missiles & Space Company, Inc.; Crown Zellerbach Corporation; and Singer-Link Data Center. My special thanks and gratitude go to my editor, Dr. Ned Chapin, for his continued assistance and patience.

J. Van Duyn

Santa Clara, California

INTRODUCTION

The purpose of this book is to provide the reader with simple, functional EDP documentation standards. It is designed to communicate and thus establish the criteria, objectives, and functions of systems and programs (whether batch or real-time mode) developed and implemented by data processing personnel. The result of this functional design is a reliable documentation product that serves as a reference for management, nonprogramming user, systems analyst, programmer, operator, and auditor.

This documentation guide, being flexible yet detailed, may be used by any computer installation since it is hardware- and software-independent.

HOW TO USE THIS BOOK

To facilitate finding specific information, the text is divided into the following section units:

BOOK/SECTION I: *General System*—for management, nonprogramming users, as well as systems analysts.
BOOK/SECTION II: *File and I/O Specifications*—for EDP professionals.
BOOK/SECTION III: *Programming Specifications*—for EDP professionals.
BOOK/SECTION IV: *Clerical Procedures*—for EDP clerks.
BOOK/SECTION V: *Audit Control Description*—for EDP control personnel.
BOOK/SECTION VI: *Operator's Instructions*—for computer operators.

Each book/section discusses a separate documentation task for a particular book (if it's a large system) or a particular section (if it's a small system). This "entity" method of having each documented phase—for example, General System—in a separate book/section provides for easier final documentation (two or more book/sections can be documented simultaneously); distribution of the relevant book/sections to the proper department/personnel (EDP personnel who have to interface on certain phases of system development should have a copy of all of the appropriate book/sections); and maintaining or updating the separate phases of the system becomes much easier.

Correlatively, each book (or section) has a title page and a detailed page of contents that indicate the topics covered in each book/section.

The indexing technique has been devised so as to convey clearly:

- The name of the system* being documented.
- The chronological order in which the system, subsystems (if any), and programs are designed, documented, and implemented.
- The group of systems the documented system is related to—for example, the Performance Profile System belongs to a group of systems under the main system of Personnel Data Base.
- Whether a certain section is the original documentation or has been revised, and if so, how many revisions that particular system has gone through and when.

Finally, each book/section is clearly labeled (e.g., *General System* [*GS*], *File and I/O Specifications* [*FS*]). Each part is designated to specify whether it is the first, second, third, etc., part of that subsection. Further, the intersections are incremented by 10 (or whatever number you wish), so that at a later date additional material can be conveniently added. To illustrate, *INV-101-GS/010-00* means (1) the name of the documented system is INVENTORY (*INV*); it is the first system (*101*) in the INVENTORY SYSTEM group to be designed, documented, and implemented; it is Book/Section I, General System (GS), (010), following the rule of assigning ID numbers to the subphases, and of the ID numbers being incremented by 10 (if a previous system existed on which the new system is [partially or wholly] based, it would first read: INV-101-GS/001-00, and *then* INV-101-GS/010-00, and both would be included in Book/Section I); and it is the documentation of a new system (*00*).

If this system is revised, then the General System, Book/Section I, will read: INV-101-GS/010-01. At the second revision the last digits will be 02, at the third revision, 03, and so on.

This comprehensive, yet simple, indexing technique makes it easy for a programmer or systems analyst to find in a documented system any specific information he or she may need on, for example, a program or file. Also, since the documentation standards are modular, it is simplicity itself to adapt or combine any parts of it. Consequently, though different installations may have different categories, by using this documentation guide, the systems analyst and programmer can still come out with effective documentation.

Note: Whenever a computer program is modified, documentation must be modified accordingly. Whenever a section or pages are added,

*See Glossary.

deleted, or changed in the documentation, the main and sectional tables of contents must be updated automatically to insure that they reflect the latest data within that book.

Here is an overview of what a complete set of new or redesigned computer system documentation consists of:

BOOK/SECTION I. *General System* describes in nontechnical language the concept of a particular system, which is to perform a specific task. It may or may not contain the Survey Report and the Feasibility Study Report. It does include a system flowchart and a narrative description of the flow of system data. It mentions the hardware used, the projected completion date, the reports generated by the system, and the programs and files (no details, however) within the system and subsystems, if there are any.

BOOK/SECTION II. *File and Input/Output Specifications* gives a detailed, functional description of the files manipulated by the system. It includes the purpose and contents of each file and the organization and sequence of files used by the program. Also, it includes the access method and the data elements/items and their characteristics. In addition, this book contains all entries describing the incoming and outgoing data. Because of the importance of the physical characteristics of the files in a system, each file processed by a program must be described fully.

BOOK/SECTION III. *Programming Specifications* discusses in detail the identification, purpose, and function(s) of each program and subprogram within that system. It includes the language, a statement of logic behind the functions of the programs, input/output definitions of all files and records, debugging procedures, and a logic flowchart for every program. Thus a skilled programmer can save some time in understanding, or "getting the hang of," programs documented in this manner. In addition, it explains to the nonprogramming user (in case the system is designed for and handled by other than computer programmers–for example, a purchase order backlog system designed for and manipulated by the purchase department) what input he must provide in order to get the desired output.

BOOK/SECTION IV. *Clerical Procedures* explains in a simple, direct manner how the printed forms are to be filled out, the departments are to be served, input is to be prepared, output balancing and exceptions are to be handled. It explains keyboard instructions and other items for nonprofessional EDP personnel.

BOOK/SECTION V. *Audit Control Description* makes available for the internal and the external auditor all the relevant sections (duplicated from the documented portions of this particular system) that the auditor needs for his work. That is, it identifies where certain data enter and exit the system, which data are passed on to other system, and the types of control records the system contains. Also, it tells how data are checked *before* and *after* processing by the computer, and the procedure for correcting errors.

BOOK/SECTION VI. *Operator's Instructions* consists of setup instructions, identification of input/output, console messages, work-flow charts, job control/monitoring procedures, schedules, special procedures, output reproduction, and other various information the computer operator and other computer machine-room personnel need for smooth, efficient operations.

By following this guidebook's simple instructions (illustrated by documented sample applications), systems analysts as well as programmers will find documentation much less of a chore than it has been. Moreover, the advantages of quality documentation are many and far-reaching. To mention a few:

1. Clarifies the concept and design of the data flow within a system or application.
2. Brings meaning to programs and files.
3. Is invaluable as a reference for programmers transferred from another project, essential as information disseminator for newly hired programmers.
4. Is the most effective technique for establishing standards in a computer facility.

The last, but nevertheless important, reason for writing clear, cohesive documentation that is understood by managers, EDP clerks, and computer operators alike is that it is the best way to "keep them happy." This, in turn, reduces one of the professional EDP occupational hazards—ulcers—among systems and programming personnel. This alone should make the task of producing legible documentation worth the effort.

DOCUMENTATION MANUAL

BOOK/SECTION I

GENERAL SYSTEM

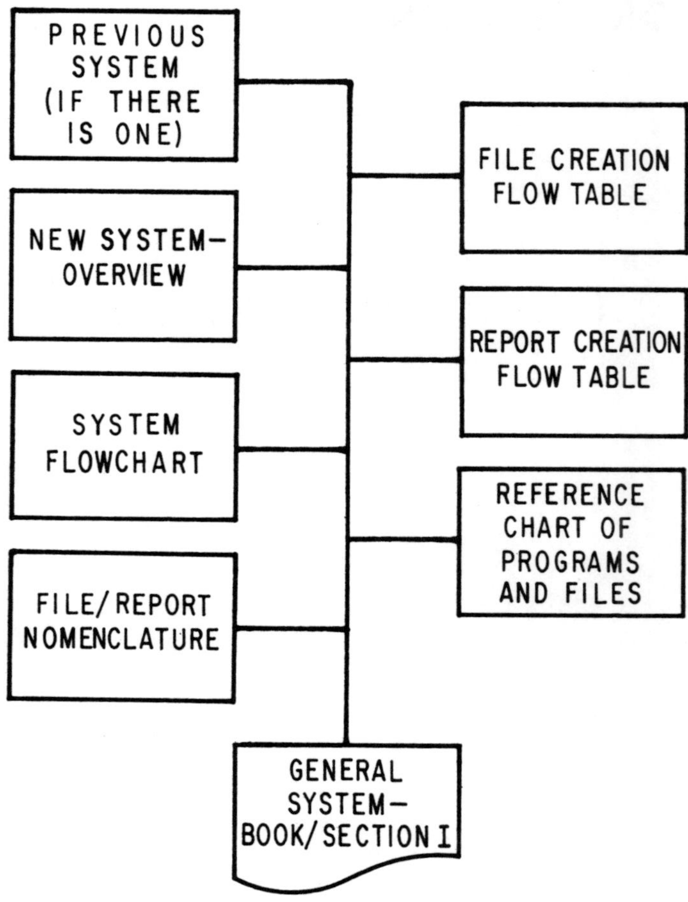

Figure 1. Organization of Book/Section I: General System

CONTENTS

GENERAL SYSTEM (XX-000-GS/000-00*)

The function of this book/section is to give management, nonprogramming users, systems analysts, and programmers an overview of a system (either a new or a redesigned old system). It provides the user with rough information about the system so he will have a general impression of what it is and how it works. Moreover, it serves as a common reference point between the user and the systems analysts and programmers at any commercial facility.

Book/section I also allows EDP professional personnel who are unfamiliar with a specific system (since they did not originate it) to get a feel for the system before getting into the details of it.

In short, the General System section is an introduction to the system. Filling in the "Documentation Checklist" form (Figure 2 is an example of it) as Book/Section I is finalized is important. It will prove to be a great time- and frustration-saver later.

PREVIOUS SYSTEM (IF THERE IS ONE) (XX-000-GS/001-00)

a. *Narrative Description* states the purpose and scope of the previous system and subsystems (if there are any). It describes in general terms the various functions performed by the major program(s) and subprogram(s) in the course of processing the input and producing the reports or displays.

b. *Input/Source Documents* describes all types of sources such as card, magnetic tape, paper tape, or disk used to input data into the system.

c. *Flowchart of All Files and Their Relation to Each Other.* A visual explanation of the files manipulated by the system.

d. *Listing of Output/Report Documents* lists the printouts produced by the system.

e. *Capabilities and Limitations* reviews specific capabilities and limitations. That is, here the designer and/or programmer indicate what is "special or different" about the system, for example, a message-switching program, a "slave" computer, an on-line tape Terabit Memory System instead of disk drive, etc.

*XX-000-GS/000-00 is in accordance with the indexing system explained in the Introduction.

NEW SYSTEM—OVERVIEW (XX-000-GS/010-00)

a. *Request and Approval Data* includes the name of the person and/or department who requested the project, the name and type of project, and the project's projected completion date. It should also include the date the analyst began the project.

b. *System Survey Report* (optional) includes in preliminary form all information necessary for management to evaluate the project, such as a description of the project and considerations bearing on the time, costs, objectives, and advantages if the project is implemented. The report should also describe the advantages of the proposed system over the present system (if one exists).

c. *Feasibility Study Report* (optional) shares many categories of data with the system survey report. However, its information should have a high degree of accuracy and reliability. This report reflects in-depth estimates of the time frame, resources, results, and costs of the project implementation. The data accumulated during the *b* and *c* phases become the basis for implementation of the system, if approved by management.

d. *Summary Description of the System* states the purpose of the system; defines briefly the file structure, organization, and sequence; describes the data elements; states the input media; and gives a narrative description of the output.

e. *Objectives and Scope* states the results produced by the system, and explains the advantages obtained by it. This section also indicates the area of the user's operations that is affected by the system.

f. *Input/Output* describes the format, content, timing, and form of the I/0 of the system. This includes peripheral equipment such as key-to-tape, key-to-disk, graphic displays, telecommunications, and so on.

g. *Hardware Configuration* lists the computer and model type and includes other relevant information such as "The hardware configuration is IBM System 360/50, 256K, two 2311 disk drives, six 2740/41 communication terminals, and one 1403 printer."

h. *Software Configuration* consists of (1) Program language(s) used for the programs and subprograms, for example, "The program language is COBOL, while the 3 subprograms are in Assembly Language"; (2) the operating system (DOS, OS, MCP, etc.); and (3) utility programs (SORT, RESORT, LINKAGE, SUPERDUMP, etc.).

i. *Operating System Required* indicates whether the particular computer system operates on OS (Operating System), DOS (Disk Operating System), MCP (Master Control Processor), SCP (System Control Processor) etc.

j. *Data Base and File Summary* gives an account of the files utilized by the system and describes the data elements/items concerning their format, size, and other characteristics.
k. *Outputs Generated by the System* lists and summarizes the data each output contains, the department/personnel who use the outputs, and the purpose of the outputs.
l. *Capabilities and Limitations* describes specific capabilities and limitations of the computer system—for example, if the input is by punched cards in free format, or the file size is limited to a certain amount of records to be stored on disk, or "only six 2260 CRT (cathode ray tube) display terminals are available."
m. *Considerations* conveys miscellanous information that has not been touched on in a previous section.

FLOW OF SYSTEM DATA (XX-000-GS/020-00)

a. *System Flowchart* is a diagram showing the flow of data through the system. It lists the input media and the various functions performed by the programs and subprograms in the course of accessing the files, processing and producing the output. The chart also indicates the contents and destination of the output (reports, graphic, display, etc.). If the system contains subsystems, there is a separate flowchart for each.
b. *Narrative Description of System Flow* is a clarification of the information in the system flowchart.

REFERENCE CHART OF PROGRAMS AND FILES (XX-000-GS/030-00)

This chart cross-references the files and shows their interrelationship to the programs that process them.

FILE CREATION FLOW TABLE (XX-000-GS/040-00)

This table indicates the name of each file, sort fields in major to minor sequence, initiator, and output.

OUTPUT CREATION FLOW TABLE (XX-000-GS-050-00)

This table indicates the names of all types of output (reports, files, etc.), the programs that produce these outputs, the input files, and the disposition of the output.

FILE/OUTPUT NOMENCLATURE (XX-000-GS/060-00)

This subsection clarifies the meaning of the file and the specific output names and acronyms.

To enhance the functionality of the manual examples, a documented sample application follows each chapter. The types of applications that are used as illustrations were selected for their wide use at commercial and noncommercial installations.

PER-101-GS/000-00*
Date
Company/Division

SAMPLE APPLICATION:

PERFORMANCE PROFILE SYSTEM—GENERAL SYSTEM

*The prefix "PER" can be either two or three letters. In this case we are using three letters for ease of identifying the system. For the index key, please see the Introduction.

PER-101-GS/000-00
Date
Company/Division

RESPONSIBLE EDP PERSONNEL

Senior Systems Analyst	(name)
Systems Analyst	(name)
Senior Programmer	(name)
Programmer	(name)
Documentation Editor	(name)
Documentation Writer	(name)

Contents

PER-101-GS/000-00
Date
Company/Division

System No. & Name: PER-101, PERFORMANCE PROFILE SYSTEM

Date: 6/17/71

Systems Analyst(s): Charles Smith & R. Dunn

User (Name & phone): Personnel Dept. X239

Items required and contained in this book/section	Yes	No	Comments (if no is checked)
Previous (computer system)		√	N.A.—No previous system
1. Request and approval data	√		
2. System survey and feasibility study reports	√		
3. General system concepts and purpose of system	√		
4. System flowchart	√		
5. Narrative description of the system flow with index to subsystems (if applicable)	√		
6. Number and names of files and their relationship to programs	√		
7. Reports generated by the system	√		
8. Hardware and software configurations	√		
9. Operating system required	√		
10. Capabilities and limitations	√		
11. Considerations		√	No special considerations in this system
12. Miscellaneous data not included above		√	None

Figure 2. Documentation Checklist

PER-101-GS/010-00
Date
Company/Division

SAMPLE

OVERVIEW

a. Request and Approval Data

1. Initiator: Director, Personnel Department.
2. Project name and type: PERFORMANCE PROFILE SYSTEM, record-keeping, nonaccounting.
3. Approved: (date). Target date given by initiator: (date).
4. Starting date:

b. System Survey Report

N.A.

c. Feasibility Study Report

Three alternatives were considered. The first was to expand the existing Payroll System Master File to include additional data and to alter the payroll system so that it would provide the desired updating ability and produce the required reports. The second was to use the Phillip Hankins Payroll System. The third alternative was to design a new system, but use the existing files, such as the Payroll Master, Savings Master, and Attendance Master and thus generate the needed reports. Subsequently the third alternative was chosen.

d. Summary Description of the System

The purpose of the Performance Profile System is to create and provide a convenient means for maintaining a large collection of information about each company employee. The system has two major files: the Master Personnel File, which contains most of the data about each employee, and the Progress File, which contains information about the employee's progress at the company. The latter file includes such items as promotion, education courses, and change in department or office. There are also four small table files that are used only when reports are generated; they greatly reduce the size of the Master Personnel File.

Input to the system is by punched cards in free format. Any of the six files may be added to or altered and a variety of reports may be generated merely by supplying the appropriate control cards as input.

PER-101-GS/010-00
Date
Company/Division

SAM

e. Objectives and Scope

The objective of the system documented herein is to produce a three-dimensional profile of each employee. This is accomplished by creating and maintaining a comprehensive, up-to-date record of the staff. All of the files can be accessed and updated by the user through the normal input stream (cards) without any systems or programming-staff assistance.

f. Hardware Configuration

IBM System 360 Model 65, minimum 72K, maximum 100K.

g. Software Configuration

The program language is COBOL, except for three subprograms—Capture, Sort, and Resort—which are in Assembly Language.

h. Operating System Required

OS/360 MVT.

j. Reports Generated by the System

1. *EMPLOYEE STATUS REPORT.* A single-page summary of pertinent information on a given employee, such as current salary, title, department, etc.
2. *JOB CLASSIFICATION REPORT.* Lists the latest job classification status.
3. *GRADE/SALARY REPORT.* Gives the latest grade and salary position.
4. *LIFE INSURANCE REPORT.* Contains status of employee life insurance.
5. *HEALTH INSURANCE REPORT.* Contains status of employee hospital insurance.
6. *CONTROL REPORT.* Gives statistical data about the run and size of the Master Personnel File and the Progress File.
7. *EXCEPTION REPORT.* Contains a listing of each run's invalid transactions. Shows which items did not process, and prints the error messages.

PER-101-GS/010-00
Date
Company/Division

Col. No.	Data Element/Item	Data Originates In	Data Used In	Size/ Units	Type	Format Example	Special Characteristics
18	Job number	Personnel file	Personnel	6	N	002300	None
19	Job title	" "	"	8	A	000450	"
20	Grade	" "	"	7	A/N	001360	"
21	Current salary	Master payroll	Wkly payroll & pers.	7	N	002470	"
22	Last review date	Personnel file	Personnel	6	N	000140	"
23	Last incr.—amt.	Master payroll	Wkly payroll & pers.	7	N	000180	"
24	Type	" "	" " "	7	A	000450	Format conventions
25	Date	" "	" " "	6	N	001360	None

NOTE: A comprehensive table of all Data Elements is in the FILE SPECIFICATIONS, Section II of the PERFORMANCE PROFILE SYSTEM.

Legend: A = alphabetic; A/N = alphanumeric; N = numeric.

Figure 3. Data Base and File Summary Table

PER-101-GS/010-00
Date
Company/Division

SAM

The first five reports are run at the request of the Personnel Department on the average of once a month. The Control and Exception Reports are generated automatically for each run, as well as printouts of any employee record or Table File altered during the run.

k. Capabilities and Limitations

Input is via 80-column standard punched cards in free format. File size is limited to 10,000 records on the 2311 disk storage device.

SAMPLE

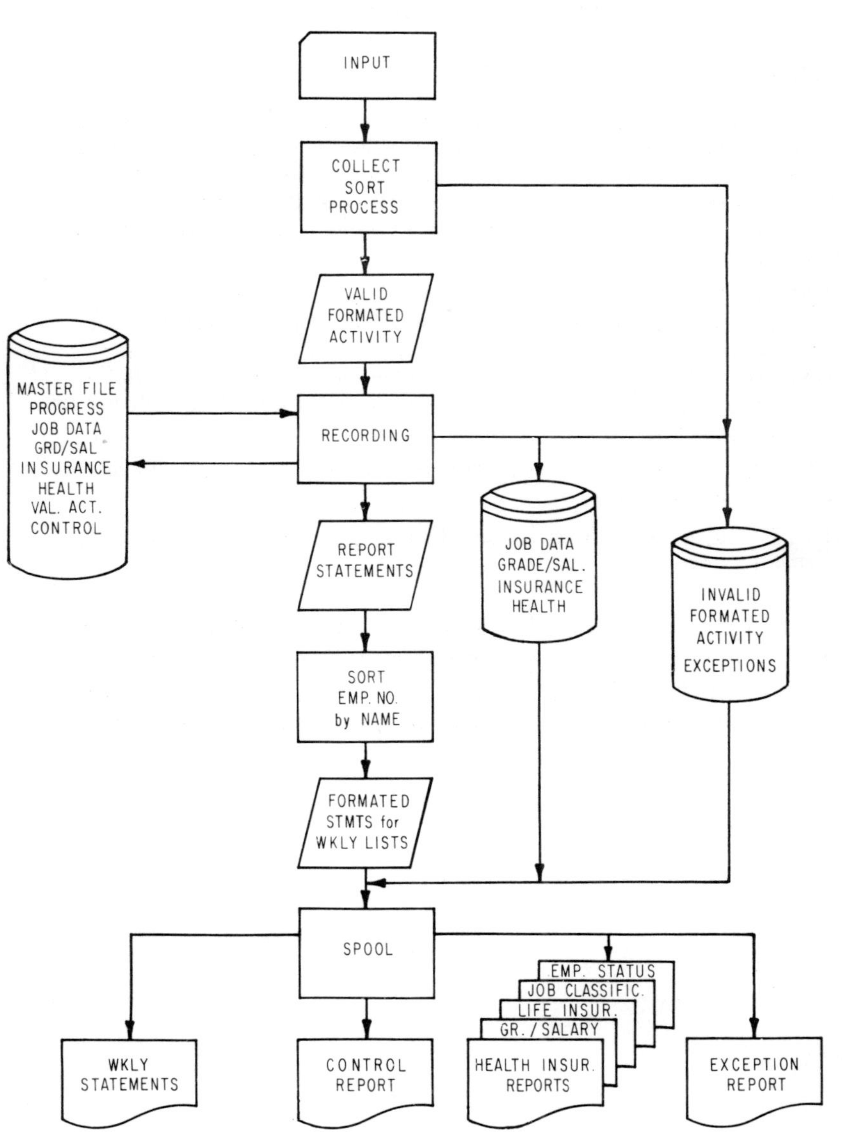

Figure 4. System Flowchart

PER-101-GS/020-00
Date
Company/Division

SAMP

FLOW OF SYSTEM DATA

Narrative Description of System Flow

a. Input consists of control cards in free form. The COLLECT-SORT-PROCESS PROGRAM is comprised of three phases: (1) the COLLECT phase accepts the input. Subsequently, one of the Assembly Language routines takes the input and breaks it out into separate transactions. (2) The data is sorted by the SORT phase, then (3) edited by the PROCESS phase. PROCESS writes out the valid or invalid formated activity.

b. RECORDING accepts all of the system's files, that is, the two major files, Master Personnel and Progress; the four table files, Job Data, Grade/Salary, Life Insurance, Health Insurance; and the Control file (all disk files) and processes them. RECORDING adds onto the Exception, writes out all the files, and generates the reports. This is done whenever there is any change or when a change is requested.

c. SORT Employee Number by Name provides the user and the employees' files weekly formated lists.

d. SPOOL gets information from Process, telling Spool when to start printing and when to stop.

Questions such as "What files are coming out?," "What is the Input/Output Sequence?," and the like are answered in Figure 6, while questions about "the variations coming into the input" are answered in the CLERICAL PROCEDURES section, Input Format, CP/030.

PER-101-GS/030-00
Date
Company/Division

SAMPLE

FILES	PUG[a]	PERE[b]	PERD[c]	PERC[d]
PER JOB(-2)	X			
PER GRADE(-2)	X			
PER INSUR(-2)	X			
PER MAST(-2)	X			
PER PROG(-2)	X			
PER HLTH (-2)	X			
PER CTL(-2)	X			
PER ACT(-2)	X			
PER STMTS.UNST	X	X	X	
PER STMTS.SORT	X	X		
PER CTLRPT	X		X	
PER JOBRPT	X		X	
PER GRDRPT	X		X	
PER INSRPT	X		X	
PER HLTHRPT	X		X	
PER EMPNRPT	X		X	X
PER ACT(0)				X
PER MAST(-1)			X	
PER MAST(0)			X	
PER PROG(-1)			X	
PER JOB(-1)			X	
PER JOB(0)			X	
PER GRADE(-1)			X	
PER GRADE(0)			X	
PER INSUR(-1)			X	
PER INSUR(0)			X	
PER HLTH(-1)			X	
PER HLTH(0)			X	
PER CTL(-1)			X	
PER CTL(0)			X	
PER ACT(0)			X	
	16	2	21	2

(PROGRAMS: PUG, PERE, PERD, PERC)

Legend:

[a]PUG A dummy program used to allocate/delete files
[b]PERE SORT Program
[c]PERD RECORDING Program
[d]PERC COLLECT/SORT/PROCESS Program

Figure 5. Quick Reference Chart of Programs and Files

PER-101-GS/040-00
Date
Company/Division

File Names	SEQUENCE			FILE OUTPUT	
	Input	Output	Initiated	Files	Reports
PER master	Social Security	Social Security	Personnel Dept., Attendance Syst., Saving Syst.		Employee status
PER progress	Social Security, History, Line	Social Security, History, Line	PER Master File, Personnel Dept.		Employee status
Health insur.	Assigned by line number	Assigned by line number	Personnel Dept.	PER Master	Health insur.
Life insur.	Assigned by line number, salary	Assigned by line number, salary	Personnel Dept.	PER Master	Life insur.
Job data	Job class code	Job class code	Personnel Dept.	PER Master	Job classification
Grade/Salary	Grade	Grade	Personnel Dept.	PER Master	Grade/Salary
Valid activity	I.D., history, line, type code, tran. code	I.D., history, line, type code, tran. code	Personnel Dept., Attendance Syst., Savings Syst.		Employee statements
Control			Recording program		Control

Figure 6. File Creation Flow Table

SAMP

PER-101-GS/050-00
Date
Company/Division

SAMPLE

Report Names	Programs	Input Files	Disposition of Reports
Employee Status	RECORDING	PER Progress	Personnel Dept.
Health Insurance	"	Health	" "
Job Classification	"	Job Data	" "
Life Insurance	"	Insurance	" "
Grade/Salary	"	Grade/Salary	" "
Control	"	Control	Auditor
Exception	PROCESS, RECORDING		Personnel Dept.

Figure 7. Report Creation Flow Table

PER-101-GS/060-00
Date
Company/Division

FILE/REPORT NOMENCLATURE

ACTIVITY/ACT	Input transactions found valid by Process and passed on to Recording program.
CONTROL/CTL	This file contains totals of daily transactions on PER Master and PER Progress files such as total active, retired, and terminated employees on Master and total Progress records.
CONTROL REPORT	Prints and totals data generated by Control File.
EXCEPTIONS REPORT	Contains a list of invalid input activity generated by Process. Also, unprocessed items generated by Recording, as well as errors found in files when posting.
GRADE/SALARY	A table file relating salary range to its corresponding grade classification and providing a salary review period to the salary.
GRADE/SALARY REPORT	Formated information generated by the Grade/Salary file. Printed only when file changes or upon request.
HEALTH/HLTH	A table file indicating amount and type of health insurance by premium.
HEALTH REPORT	Formated information generated by Health file. Printed only when file changes or upon request.
INSURANCE	A table file correlating salary to life insurance amount and deduction.
JOB CLASSIFICATION REPORT	Formated information generated by Job Data file. Printed only when file changes or upon request.

PER-101-GS/060-00
Date
Company/Division

SAMPLE

JOB DATA	A table file containing a description of all job classifications.
LIFE INSURANCE REPORT	Formated information generated by Insurance File. Printed only when file changes or upon request.
PER MASTER	One of the major files. It is a data base for every employee. It contains current status of nonstatic information and a summary of static data.
PER PROGRESS	The second major file. It contains a history of nonstatic data such as grade, promotion, department, and shift changes, credit or noncredit courses taken, and so on.
STATUS REPORT	Presents comprehensive information about personnel from PER Master and PER Progress files. Printed only when there is a change in the files or upon request.

BOOK/SECTION II

FILE AND I/O SPECIFICATIONS

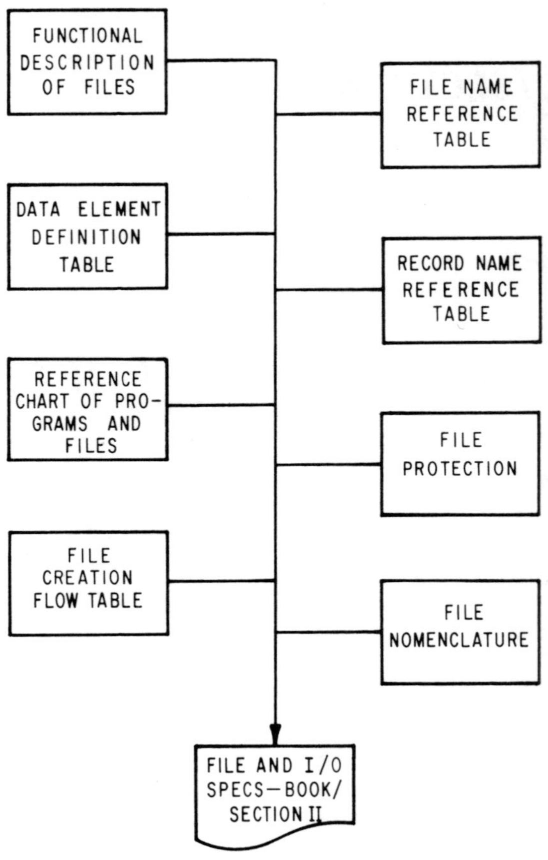

Figure 8. Organization of Book/Section II: File and I/O Specifications

CONTENTS

FILE AND I/O SPECIFICATIONS (XX-000-FS/000-00*)

This book/section gives a detailed description of the files manipulated by the system. It includes the purpose, contents, and organization of the files; the storage media; file ID; access methods; labeling conventions; blocking factors; record structure; and update cycle, in addition to the data elements and their characteristics. Each and every file in a system must be described and included in the File Specifications.

FUNCTIONAL DESCRIPTION OF FILES: THEIR PURPOSE AND CONTENT (XX-000-FS/010-00)

a. *Background Information* is a narrative description of the file. It defines the file's purpose and content, which system it belongs to; its organization and sequence; and its labeling convention. Also, it should include the file name and the file ID tags, file size for example, "8,000 records, 6 items of data per record."; file function, for example, "This is a temporary file which stores 'Pass Through' data for a Purchase Order (PO) until all of the data for the PO has been corrected."

b. *Timing.* States the frequency of the file running–for example, "Once a week"–and how often the file is updated–for example, "Twice a month."

c. *File Security.* Clarifies who has access, at what time, and the priority established. This is especially important point when there is a multiple system with multiple users who want the privacy of access to file data rigorously enforced.

d. *Storage Medium.* Defines the file device (punched cards, magnetic tape, disk, etc.).

e. *Access Method.* Explains whether the file organization is sequential, indexed sequential, random (direct access), inverted file, multilist structure, or complex ring.

f. *Key Fields.* Describes the key that determines the sequence by which the file is accessed and includes the File Name, Field Size, Sequence, and where used (the last item is optional). For example, "The Sort Key for this file is: Facility; PO Serial (last 2), Major; PO Serial (first 3), Major; Requestor, Major; Item

*XX-000-FS/000-00 is in accordance with the indexing, system explained in the Introduction.

Code; Major, Trailer Indicator, Minor." Another example: "PO serial numbers are assigned in sequence within each Requestor, so the serial and Requestor are scrambled in the Sort Key to spread additions evenly throughout the disk file."

g. *Programs Using the File.* States which program(s) process the file.

h. *I/O Definitions, Layouts of All Files, and I/O Records.* Discusses the format and characteristics of the input to the system, that is, what type of input or source documents are required–for example, control or data cards, tapes or disk. In addition, it states which input creates another file or files, for example, "The input data to Grade/Salary file–initiated in Personnel Department–is passed on to PER Master file."

   Also, the output of the system is defined–that is, reports, other printed documents, files, printout or CRT (cathode ray tube) display, etc., created by the system.

   Layouts of all files are given via File Record Layout and File Specifications on preprinted forms such as the IBM System 360 File or Data Record Layout (see Figure 13). The disk (with format and storage limit) can be mentioned here, along with the I/O records, which utilizes the IBM 360 data record layout (Figure 13). This preprinted form is a visual explanation of the record name, field label, length-variability, input form arrangement, logical order of the data, field description, and field usage.

i. *Data Element Reference Table.* Gives a comprehensive picture of the data elements by listing the data name, data label, classification, justification, length-variability, code value, and so forth. (see XX-000-FS/020-00, Figure 9, for a sample form of this matrix chart).

j. *Record Sequence.* Indicates whether the record type is fixed or of variable length.

k. *Retention Characteristics.* Before purging, describes the time or number of cycles the file or record is to be retained, and where. For example, "Master records containing error fields will be kept on the (Master) file for immediate corrections. A record which has remained in error for 9 days will be dropped from the file."

l. *Reconstruction.* Describes the procedure for reconstructing the file, if necessary. For example, "The Antioch Inventory Control System Master File is copied onto a tape at the beginning of each month. In the event of disk failure, the tape can be copied back to the disk and the necessary week's rerun."

m. *Estimated Volume or the Number of Records.* Gives the average number of records presently within the file–the growing and diminishing file, seasonal (swing articles) file, etc.

n. *Estimated Peak Volume.* Shows the pattern of growth of the records by stating the probable peak number of records within the file; that is, it is a high-activity indicator.

o. *Volatility.* States the dynamic changes that can be expected under certain conditions: a flip-flop may be volatile or data in a storage device (e.g., a magnetic tape unit) cannot be recovered when lost power is restored.

DATA ELEMENT REFERENCE TABLE (XX-000-FS/020-00)

See Figure 9.

QUICK REFERENCE CHART OF PROGRAMS AND FILES (XX-000-FS/030-00)

This chart cross-references the files and any file generation within the system with the programs that process them. (This chart is a duplicate of GS/030, Figure 5.)

FILE CREATION FLOW TABLE (XX-000-FS/040-00)

This table indicates the name of each file, the input/output sequence (sort fields in major to minor sequence) where the file was initiated, and the file output (reports and files). This is a duplicate of GS/040, (Figure 6).

FILE NAME REFERENCE TABLE (XX-000-FS/050-00)

This table cross-references the following names for each file: Common Name, Common Abbreviation, COBOL FD (File Description) Name, DS (Data Set) Name, and if applicable, Copy/Program Library Name.

RECORD NAME REFERENCE TABLE (XX-000-FS/060-00)

This table cross-references the records' names, such as: Common Name, Common Abbreviation, Data Record Name from FD, and Copy/Program Library Name, lining them up with the File Name (in the first column).

FILE PROTECTION (XX-000-FS/070-00)

This subsection indicates the checkpoints for data control, and/or where the data passes through the system. See Book/Section V, Audit Control, for details on data control.

FILE NOMENCLATURE (XX-000-FS/080-00)

This subsection clarifies the meaning of file names and acronyms and describes briefly their data content.

Column Number	Data Name	Data Label	Description	Data Originates In	Data Used In	Type	Justific.	Length Variability	Code Value	Data Appears In	Special Characteristics
1	Social Security	SS	Social Security	Source document	PER master file	N/D	L	F	3	Emp. status report	None

Legend: *Type,* A = alphabetic, A/N = alphanumeric, N = numeric; *Justification,* L = left justified, R = right justified, F = full field; *Length Variability,* F = fixed length, V = variable length; *Base,* B = binary, D = decimal, F = floating point; *Code Values,* 1 = technical, 2 = business, 3 = personal, 4 = general.

Figure 9. Data Element Reference Table (XX-000-FS/020-00)

PDA-104-FS/000-02*
Date
Company/Division

SAMPLE APPLICATION:

PROCUREMENT (AUTOMATIC) DATA ACQUISITION SYSTEM— FILE AND I/O SPECIFICATIONS

*For the index key, please see the Introduction.

PDA-104-FS/000-02
Date
Company/Division

SAMPL

Contents

PDA-104-FS/000-02
Date
Company/Division

SAMPLE

System No. & Name: PDA-104, PROCUREMENT (AUTOMATIC) DATA ACQUISITION SYSTEM   Date:

Programming Group Leader: (name)   Computer Programmer: (name)

Items required and contained in this book/section	Yes	No	Comments (if no is checked)
1. File Background & Characteristics	√		
2. Storage Device	√		
3. File Organization & Code	√		
4. Sort/Field Keys	√		
5. Labeling Conventions	√		
6. Record Structure	√		
7. Current Volume & Peak	√		
8. Update Cycle	√		
9. Retention Periods	√		
10. Data Element Description	√		
11. Output Description	√		

Figure 10. Documentation Checklist

PDA-104-FS/010-02
Date
Company/Division

SAMP

FUNCTIONAL DESCRIPTION OF FILES: THEIR PURPOSE AND CONTENT

Background Information

The present or revised Procurement (Automatic) Data Acquisition (PDA)* real-time system on the IBM System/360 computer consists of data banks of purchase orders, receiving memos, and inventory records. The system processes transactions from remote input terminals in Procurement Operating areas, updating the data banks so that current status information is available to personnel plant-wide, using IBM System/360. Data transmission is limited in the number of characters transmitted, and some batch processing of data is necessary. The file is updated from batch information once a week.

Purchase order data is prepared for the file after buyer placement through dispatching the completed purchase request document from six major areas of buying activity to a central data input function called Procurement Document Control. IBM 2740 Terminals are used to input information to the IBM System/360.

It is only after purchase order data enters the file from this central data collection point that purchase order information is available for inquiry and other computer processing to accounts payable, inventory control, and financial committment accountability systems.

When material arrives at one of the three receiving docks, an inquiry device is used to request an instant receiving memo tab card, which is created on-line at the receiving dock. An extensive audit is completed using a purchase request copy that is maintained on each dock in a manual file. Upon completion of the audit, the receiving memo tab card is inserted in a remote data terminal, thus authenticating the receipt at LMSC. At this point, the receiving memo data becomes available to anyone inquiring about the status of a purchase order. The data is processed to the accounts payable system for automatic payment. The material and the receiving memo package subsequently moves through receiving inspection stations and the same receiving memo tab card is used to transmit on remote data input devices the movement of the material through receiving inspection. The receiving memo receives a final closure transmission upon delivery to stores or for direct-delivery items as it enters the transportation system.

*Through the courtesy of Lockheed Missiles & Space Company, Inc. (LMSC), Sunnyvale, California.

PDA-104-FS/010-02
Date
Company/Division

SAMPLE

PDA has enabled procurement to respond most efficiently and timely to the demands for status information. It also speeds the vital flow of material upon receipt. Approximately 5,000 purchase orders, 6,000 receiving memos, and 33,000 store transactions enter the system each week, and the data is constantly feeding other vital material and financial computer systems. The on-line file contains over 60,000 purchase orders and 130,000 inventory records, with 21,000 inquiries per week for information.

The system includes the following files:

1. *The PDA MASTER FILE.* This file consists of:
   (1) A simple record consisting of a Master Record only (about 80% of the file).
   (2) A complex record consisting of a Master Record and a Trailer Record.

   The PDA Master File contains Purchase Requests (PRs), Changed Purchase Requests (CPRs), Purchase Orders (POs), and Delivery Requests (DRs).

   DRs are stored on file in a skeleton form until a record is sent to PDA 4C and the completed DR (that is, simple purchase order) is returned.

   Master Records containing error fields are kept on the file for immediate corrections. A record that has remained in error for nine days is dropped from the file. POs are dropped from the file 10 days after material closure.

   The sort key for this file is:

Facility	Major
PO Serial (last 2)	Major
PO Serial (first 3)	Major
Requestor	Major
Item Code	Major
Trailer Indicator	Minor

   PO serial numbers are assigned in sequence within each Requestor, so the Serial and Requestor are scrambled in the sort key to spread additions evenly throughout the disk file.

2. *The PDA RM FILE.* The input to this file is material received at the dock. (Exceptions to this rule include Receiving Memos [RM] for receipt of service or tooling.)

   As the material is moved, the RM location code is changed. The

PDA-104-FS/010-02
Date
Company/Division

SAMPL

RM is closed when the material is either received in stores or returned to the vendor. When the sum of the quantities received in stores for all of the RMs against one purchase order equals the quantity ordered, the Purchase Order is materially closed.

Ten days after a Purchase Order is materially closed, the Purchase Order and all of its RMs are purged from the file.

The sort key for this file is:

Facility
Requestor
PO Serial (last 3)
PO Serial (first 2)
Item Code
RM Number
Split Code

3. *The PASS THROUGH DATA FILE.* This is a temporary file that stores "pass through" data for a PO until all of the data for that PO has been corrected.

   The term "pass through" has been derived because this data is needed by PDA 4D, but is not on the PDA Master.

   This file consists of 20 records set up permanently with sort keys of 01 through 20.

   A table setup in the linkage section stores the applicable PO Sort Key with its pointer to the PASS THROUGH DATA FILE. This pointer remains only until all of the data fields on the PO Master and the PASS THROUGH DATA record are corrected.

   All pointers are destroyed every night. Therefore, all POs should be corrected immediately or the PASS THROUGH DATA will have to be re-input.

4. *MASTER AUDIT FILE.* This file is updated by the finance partition and is accessed by the PDA real-time system only to validate Charge Numbers and to pick up Prime Contract Numbers and Priority Ratings.

   Two types of records the PDA system is concerned with are: Record Code 09, Work Authority Records; and Record Code 05, Project Records. The Work Authority Record is used to validate a Charge Number.

left short

The Work Authority Record's sort key is:

File ID (Constant "C")	Major
Record Sequence (Constant "6")	Major
Major Class	Major
Work Order	Major
Work Authority	Major
Minor Class	Major
15 Spaces	Major
Record Type (Constant "09")	Minor

After validation the Project Record must be accessed to pick up the Contract Number and Priority Rating. The sort key for the Project Record is:

File ID (Constant "C")	Major
Record Sequence (Constant "6")	Major
Major Class	Major
Project Number	Major
20 Spaces	Major
Record Type (Constant "05")	Minor

5. *The 5A INVENTORY FILE.* This file is updated by PDA 4B when:

(1) An inventory PR or PO is added to the PDA 4B Master File. The PR/PO number must be moved to one of the 10 spaces for open purchasing documents on the 5A record for that part.

(2) Material is received in stores. It must be added to the on-hand quantity on the 5A record for that part.

The sort key for the 5A Inventory File is:

Part Number	Major
IAC	Minor

a. Storage Media are two 2311 disk drives.
b. Access Method is both sequential and random.
c. Sort/Key Fields: see section 2-5.
d. Programs Using the Files: CAPTURE/SORT/EDIT, UPDATE, DAILY REPORT GENERATOR, WEEKLY REPORT GENERATOR, and many subprograms.
e. Source Documents: Purchase Requests, Changed Purchase Requests, Purchase Orders, Receiving Memos (RMs), Charge Numbers, Prime Contract Numbers, Priority Ratings, and Delivery Requests.

PDA-104-FS/010-02
Date
Company/Division

SAMPL

f. Output Documents: Reports generated by the programs are: Purchase Order/Delivery Status (daily); Purchase Order Summary (weekly); and Purchase Request/Receiving Memo (on request). These reports are used by Procurement, Manufacturing, Accounts Payable, Inventory Control, and Financial Commitment Accountability.

   The same latest status information is available to the above departments on their inquiry display devices.

g. Data Element References: See Figures 11, 12, and 14.

h. Record Layout Form: See Figure 13.

i. Retention Characteristics: Any record that has remained in error for nine days is dropped from the file. Purchase Orders and their Receiving Memos are dropped from the file 10 days after material closure.

   All report files are to be scratched as soon as the report is printed.

A FREE FORM DATA ELEMENT REFERENCE TABLE

PDA-104-FS/020-02

BLOCK NUMBER	BLOCK DATA NAME	PROGRAM DATA NAME	PICTURE	SIZE	4B COLUMN	P86-12 COLUMN PR	P86-12 COLUMN PO
I01	DELETE INDICATOR	DELETE	X	1	1		
	DELETE INDICATOR - WHEN A DELETE TRANSACTION IS INPUT TO THE FILE A "D" IS ENTERED IN THE FIRST POSITION OF THE RECORD. THIS SAME RECORD MAY BE SET UP IMMEDIATELY.						
I02	FACILITY	FACILITY	X	1	2	1	1
	FACILITY - ON ALL INPUT RECORDS THE SYSTEM WILL ENTER A 1 (ONE) IN THE RECORD.						
05	PO SERIAL (LAST 2)	PO-SERIAL-L2	XX	2	4	7	7
	SEQUENCE NO. WITHIN REQUESTOR CODE ASSIGNED MECHANICALLY OR MANUALLY TO ASSURE DUPLICATION DOES NOT OCCUR.						
05	PO SERIAL (FIRST 3)	PO-SERIAL-F3	X(3)	3	7	5	5
	SEQUENCE NO. WITHIN REQUESTOR CODE ASSIGNED MECHANICALLY OR MANUALLY TO ASSURE DUPLICATION DOES NOT OCCUR.						
05	REQUESTOR CODE	REQUESTOR	X	1	8	4	4
	IDENTIFICATION OF ORGANIZATION/GROUP REQUESTING MATERIAL						
05	ITEM CODE	ITEM	X	1	9	10	10
	ALL ORIGINAL P.O. NUMBERS END IN ZERO. WHEN A P.O. SPLIT IS REQUIRED A NUMBER IS ASSIGNED TO MAKE IT UNIQUE.						
I03	TRAILER	TRAILER	X	1	10	12	12
	THIS IS AN INDICATOR WITH THE FOLLOWING MEANINGS: 0 = MASTER RECORD WITH NO TRAILER 1 = MASTER RECORD WITH TRAILER 2 = TRAILER RECORD (SEE BLOCK I37)						

Figure 11. PDA Master File. Through the courtesy of LMSC.

SAMPLE

PDA-104-FS/020-02

BLOCK NUMBER	BLOCK DATA NAME	PROGRAM DATA NAME	PICTURE	SIZE	4B COLUMN	P86-12 COLUMN PR	P86-12 COLUMN PO
I04	RECORD STATUS	REC-STATUS	X	1	11	13	13

RECORD STATUS - A ONE DIGIT INDICATOR THAT SHOWS THE FOLLOWING:

NOTE: REFERENCE PAGE 5.3.1 FOR DEFINITION OF INVENTORY AND NONINVENTORY IAC'S

0 = CPR RECORD FROM D24.

1 = INVALID INVENTORY PR RECORD. ONE OR MORE DATA FIELDS ARE IN ERROR OR MANDATORY FIELDS MISSING.

2 = VALID INVENTORY PR RECORD. ALL MANDATORY FIELDS ARE PRESENT OR FIELD ERRORS HAVE BEEN CORRECTED.

3 = INVALID NONINVENTORY PR RECORD. ONE OR MORE DATA FIELDS ARE IN ERROR OR MANDATORY FIELDS ARE MISSING.

4 = VALID NONINVENTORY PR. ALL MANDATORY FIELDS ARE PRESENT OR FIELD ERRORS HAVE NOW BEEN CORRECTED.

5 = INVALID DR RECORD (MANUAL). ONE OR MORE DATA FIELDS ARE IN ERROR OR MANDATORY FIELDS ARE MISSING.

6 = VALID DR RECORD (MANUAL) ALL MANDATORY FIELDS ARE PRESENT OR FIELD ERRORS HAVE NOW BEEN CORRECTED.

7 = INVALID PO RECORD.

S = VALID "SIMPLE" PO RECORD. THIS MAY BE INPUT WITH A 530, 540 OR 550 TRANSACTION OR SYSTEM ASSIGNED IF NOT IN INPUT RECORD.

C = VALID "COMPLETE" PO RECORD. THIS MAY BE INPUT WITH A 530 OR 540 TRANSACTION.

BLOCK NUMBER	BLOCK DATA NAME	PROGRAM DATA NAME	PICTURE	SIZE	4B COLUMN	P86-12 COLUMN PR	P86-12 COLUMN PO
	FILLER	FILLER		1	12		
I05	FIELD ERROR COUNT	ERR-COUNT	S9	1	13		

FIELD ERROR COUNT - THE NUMERIC COUNT OF THE NUMBER OF FIELDS WITH INVALID DATA OR MISSING MANDATORY DATA IN THE MASTER RECORD, THE TRAILER RECORD, OR THE PASS THROUGH RECORD.

Figure 11. PDA Master File (cont.). Through the courtesy of LMSC.

SAMP

BLOCK NUMBER	BLOCK DATA NAME	PROGRAM DATA NAME	PICTURE	SIZE	4B COLUMN	P86-12 COLUMN PR	P86-12 COLUMN PO
I06	ACTIVITY DATE	ACTIVITY-DATE	S9(4)	4	17		
	ACTIVITY DATE - THE MANUFACTURING DAY A RECORD IS FIRST ENTERED ON THE FILE, OR A CHANGE IS MADE TO ANY FIELD ON THE RECORD.						
I07	ACTIVITY DAY OF WEEK	ACTIVITY-DAY	S9	1	18		
	ACTIVITY DAY OF WEEK - THIS IS NUMERIC EQUIVALENT OF DAY OF WEEK, AS MON. = 1; TUES. = 2, ETC. CHANGED IN CONJUNCTION WITH ACTIVITY DATE (BLOCK I06).						
I08	ACTIVITY TIME	ACTIVITY-TIME	X(6)	6	24		
	ACTIVITY TIME - THE HOUR, MINUTE, AND SECOND AN ACTIVITY OCCURS. CHANGED IN CONJUNCTION WITH ACTIVITY DATE (BLOCK I06).						
I09	DATE OF LAST ACTION	LAST-ACTION-DATE	X(6)	6	30		
	DATE OF LAST ACTION - THE CALENDAR DATE, MONTH, DAY, AND YEAR A RECORD IS ESTABLISHED ON THE FILE. IT IS CHANGED TO THE CURRENT DATE EACH TIME THE RECORD STATUS (BLOCK I04) IS CHANGED OR A 570 CHANGE IS PROCESSED.						
I10	MATERIAL CLOSURE	MATL-CLOSE	X	1	31	15	15
	MATERIAL CLOSURE - WHEN THE STORES QUANTITY TO UO EQUALS THE SUM OF THE QUANTITIES OF THE PROMISE SCHEDULES AN "M" IS ENTERED IN THIS FIELD. TEN DAYS FROM THE DATE THIS INDICATOR IS PUT ON THE FILE, THE RECORD IS PURGED.						
I11	FINANCIAL CLOSURE	FIN-CLOSE	X	1	32	15	15
	FINANCIAL CLOSURE - WHEN ALL PAYMENTS TO A SUPPLIER AGAINST A GIVEN PO HAVE BEEN MADE, THE P30 PROGRAM SENDS A RECORD TO P86. AN "F" INDICATOR IS THEN ENTERED IN THIS FIELD.						

Figure 11. PDA Master File (cont.). Through the courtesy of LMSC.

PDA-104-FS/020-02

BLOCK NUMBER	BLOCK DATA NAME	PROGRAM DATA NAME	PICTURE	SIZE	4B COLUMN	P86-12 COLUMN PR	P86-12 COLUMN PO
I35	DELETE INDICATOR	DELETE	X	1	1		
	DELETE INDICATOR - WHEN A DELETE TRANSACTION IS INPUT TO THE FILE A "D" IS ENTERED IN THE FIRST POSITION OF THE RECORD. AFTER DELETION THE SAME PO CAN BE SET UP IMMEDIATELY.						
I36	FACILITY	FACILITY	X	1	2	1	1
	FACILITY - SYSTEM EMITTED 1 IN EVERY RECORD.						
05	PO SERIAL (LAST 2)	PO-SERIAL-L2	XX	2	4	7	7
	SEQUENCE NO. WITHIN REQUESTOR CODE ASSIGNED MECHANICALLY OR MANUALLY TO ASSURE DUPLICATION DOES NOT OCCUR.						
05	PO SERIAL (FIRST 3)	PO-SERIAL-F3	X(3)	3	7	5	5
	SEQUENCE NO. WITHIN REQUESTOR CODE ASSIGNED MECHANICALLY OR MANUALLY TO ASSURE DUPLICATION DOES NOT OCCUR.						
05	REQUESTOR CODE	REQUESTOR	X	1	8	4	4
	IDENTIFICATION OF ORGANIZATION/GROUP REQUESTING MATERIAL						
05	ITEM CODE	ITEM	X	1	9	10	10
	ALL ORIGINAL P.O. NUMBERS END IN ZERO. WHEN A P.O. SPLIT IS REQUIRED A NUMBER IS ASSIGNED TO MAKE IT UNIQUE.						
I37	TRAILER	TRAILER	X	1	10	12	12
	TRAILER - SYSTEM EMITTED 2 IN EACH TRAILER RECORD.						

Figure 12. PDA Trailer File. Through the courtesy of LMSC.

BLOCK NUMBER	BLOCK DATA NAME	PROGRAM DATA NAME	PICTURE	SIZE	4B COLUMN	P86-12 COLUMN PR	P86-12 COLUMN PO
70	FUNDING AUTHORIZED	FUND-AUTHORIZED	S9(8)V99	10	20		499
	THE TOTAL VALUE AUTHORIZED TO START PROCUREMENT ACTION						
138	999 RM COUNT (CONSIGNMENT)	999-RM-COUNT	S9	1	21	661	661
	999 RM COUNT (CONSIGNMENT)—A COUNTER, 1-9 OF THE NUMBER OF RM 423 TRANSACTIONS TO THIS FILE. 423 TRANSACTIONS ARE ALWAYS CONSIGNMENT RM'S WITH AN RM NUMBER XXX999.						
82	TWX INDICATOR	TWX-INDIC	X	1	22	791	791
	TWX INDICATOR - WHEN A NUMERIC 1 APPEARS IN THIS FIELD THE 4D SYSTEM WILL EXCLUDE THIS PO FROM THE SUPPLIER AUTOMATIC FOLLOWUP SYSTEM.						
60L	TWX NUMBER	TWX-NO	X(12)	12	34		
	TWX NUMBER - THE TWX ADDRESS/TELEPHONE NUMBER OF THE SELLER						
I39	FAMSCO	FAMSCO	XX	2	36	81	81
	FAMSCO - AN "F" INDICATOR FOR 1-2 SCHEDULES INPUT FROM D24 WITH PR RECORDS ONLY. IT IS ALSO PRINTED ON THE PR DOCUMENT						
67	TOOL CODE	TOOL	X	1	37		334
	TOOL CODE - A CODE INDICATING THE SUPPLIER HAS TOOLING AT HIS FACILITY. BLANK = NONE						
17	ATPM	ATPM	X(7)	7	44	234	
	ATPM - AUTHORIZATION TO PURCHASE OR MANUFACTURE (ATPM) IS THE DOCUMENT NUMBER OF THE AUTHORITY TO SUPPLY MATERIAL NOT SPECIFIED IN THE PRIME CONTRACT.						

Figure 12. PDA Trailer File (cont.). Through the courtesy of LMSC.

PDA-104-FS/020-02

BLOCK NUMBER	BLOCK DATA NAME	PROGRAM DATA NAME	PICTURE	SIZE	4B COLUMN	P86-12 COLUMN PR	P86-12 COLUMN PO
18	SECURITY	SECURITY	X	1	45	241	234
	SECURITY INDICATES THE LEVEL OF SECURITY CLASSIFICATION OF THE MATERIAL OR PARTS ON A PO.						
19	BLUE PRINT	BLUE-PRINT	X	1	46	242	
	BLUE PRINT - INDICATOR MEANING PRINTS ARE REQUIRED						
22	SEGMENT-EJA-EJT	SEG-EJA-EJT	X(16)	16	62	263	242
	SEGMENT EJA ETC. - THE LMSC INTERNAL DOCUMENT NUMBER AUTHORIZING THE PROCUREMENT OF PARTS OR MATERIAL.						
29	RESALE CODE	RESALE	X	1	63	317	
	RESALE CODE - A CODE THAT SAYS THIS ITEM WILL BE RESOLD AND NOT CONSUMED BY LMSC.						
30	PRIORITY RATING	PRIORITY-RATING	X(4)	4	67	318	
	A CODE APPLIED TO SUCH GOVERNMENT CONTRACT AUTHORIZING LMSC TO PROCURE MATERIALS BY PRIORITY OF CONTRACT IMPORTANCE TO THE DEFENSE OF THE UNITED STATES.						
30A	PRIORITY CODE	PRIORITY	XX	2	69	658	658
	PRIORITY CODE - A CODE AUTHORIZED BY THE NAVY TO ESTABLISH PRIORITY FOR PR, PO AND MATERIAL PROCESSING.						
21	DELIVER TO	DELIVER-TO	X(18)	18	87	244	236
	DELIVER TO - THE LMSC INTERNAL DELIVER TO POINT						

Figure 12. PDA Trailer File (cont.). Through the courtesy of LMSC.

PDA-104-FS/010-02 SAMPLE
Date
Company/Divison

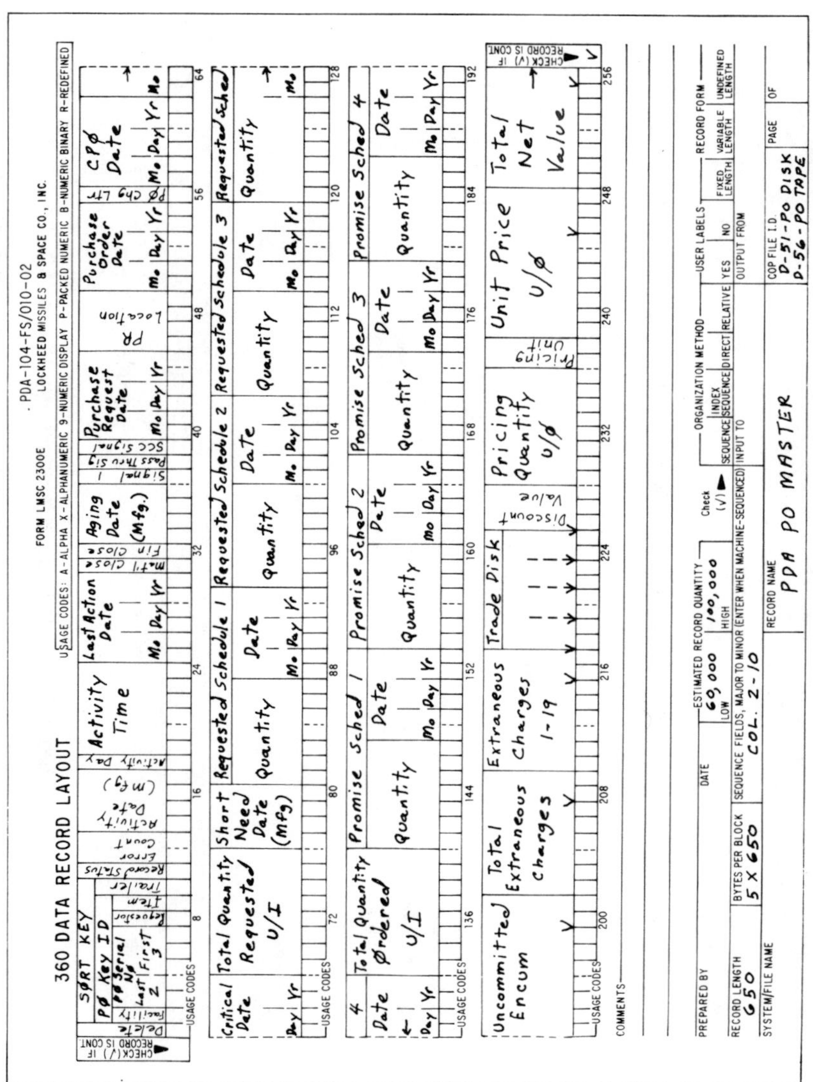

360 DATA RECORD LAYOUT
FORM LMSC 2300E
PDA-104-FS/010-02
LOCKHEED MISSILES & SPACE CO., INC.
USAGE CODES: A-ALPHA X-ALPHANUMERIC 9-NUMERIC DISPLAY P-PACKED NUMERIC B-NUMERIC BINARY R-REDEFINED

SORT KEY — PO Key ID: Delete, Facility, PO Serial No (Last 2, First 3), Requestor, Item, Trailer, Record Status, Error Count, Activity Date (Mfg), Activity Day, Activity Time, Last Action Date (Mo Day Yr), Mat'l Close, Fin Close, Aging Date (Mfg.), Signal 1, Pass Thru Sig, SCC Signal, Purchase Request Date (Mo Day Yr), PR Location, Purchase Order Date (Mo Day Yr), PO Chg Ltr, CPO Date (Mo Day Yr), Mo (8, 16, 24, 32, 40, 48, 56, 64)

Critical Date (Day Yr), Total Quantity Requested U/I, Short Need Date (Mfg), Requested Schedule 1 (Quantity, Date Mo Day Yr), Requested Schedule 2 (Quantity, Date Mo Day Yr), Requested Schedule 3 (Quantity, Date Mo Day Yr), Requested Sched 4 (Quantity, Mo) (72, 80, 88, 96, 104, 112, 120, 128)

4 Date (Day Yr), Total Quantity Ordered U/I, Promise Sched 1 (Quantity, Date Mo Day Yr), Promise Sched 2 (Quantity, Date Mo Day Yr), Promise Sched 3 (Quantity, Date Mo Day Yr), Promise Sched 4 (Quantity, Date Mo Day Yr) (136, 144, 152, 160, 168, 176, 184, 192)

Uncommitted Encum, Total Extraneous Charges, Extraneous Charges 1-19, Trade Disk, Discount Value, Pricing Quantity U/O, Pricing Unit, Unit Price U/O, Total Net Value (200, 208, 216, 224, 232, 240, 248, 256)

CHECK (✓) IF RECORD IS CONT.
USAGE CODES
COMMENTS

PREPARED BY | DATE | ESTIMATED RECORD QUANTITY: LOW 60,000, HIGH 100,000 | Check (✓) | ORGANIZATION METHOD: SEQUENCE, INDEX SEQUENCE, DIRECT, RELATIVE | USER LABELS: YES, NO | RECORD FORM: FIXED LENGTH, VARIABLE LENGTH, UNDEFINED LENGTH
RECORD LENGTH 650 | BYTES PER BLOCK 5 X 650 | SEQUENCE FIELDS, MAJOR TO MINOR (ENTER WHEN MACHINE-SEQUENCED) COL. 2-10 | INPUT TO | OUTPUT FROM
SYSTEM/FILE NAME | RECORD NAME PDA PO MASTER | COP FILE I.D. D-51-PO DISK, D-56-PO TAPE | PAGE | OF

Figure 13. 360 Data Record Layout. Lockheed Aircraft Corporation.

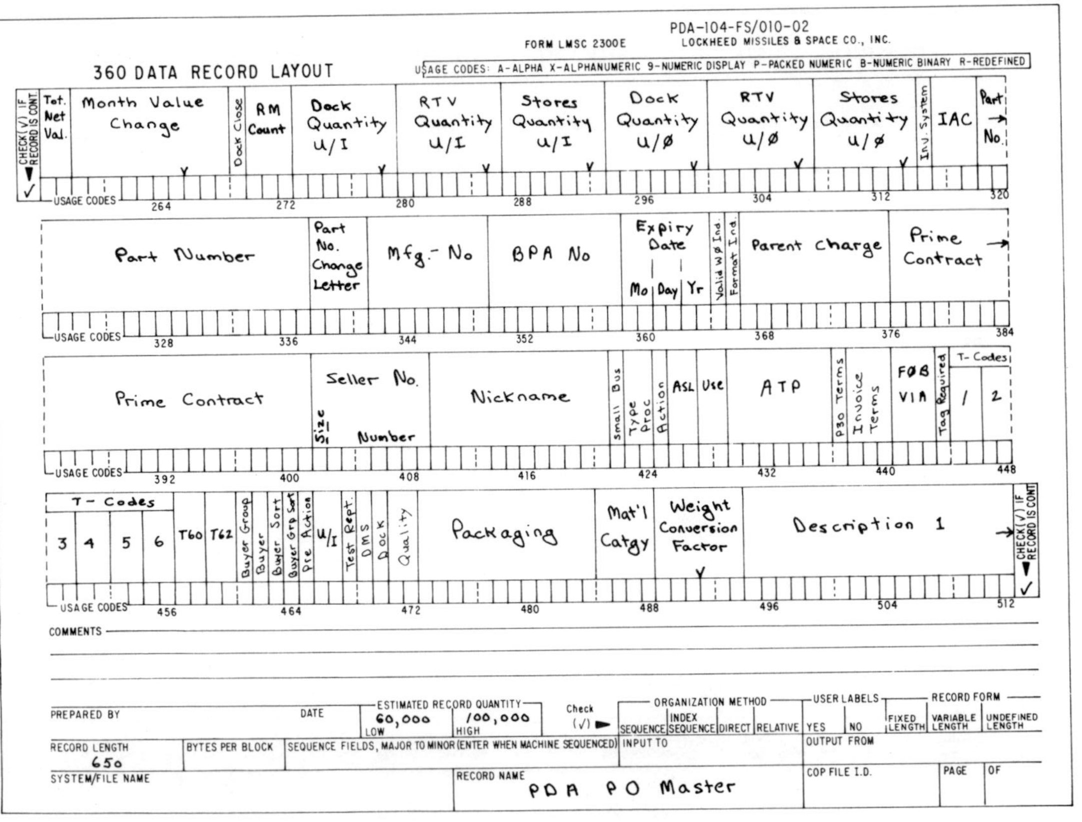
PDA-104-FS/010-02
FORM LMSC 2300E
LOCKHEED MISSILES & SPACE CO., INC.
360 DATA RECORD LAYOUT
USAGE CODES: A-ALPHA X-ALPHANUMERIC 9-NUMERIC DISPLAY P-PACKED NUMERIC B-NUMERIC BINARY R-REDEFINED

CHECK (✓) IF RECORD IS CONT | Tot. Net Val. | Month Value Change | Dock Close | RM Count | Dock Quantity U/I | RTV Quantity U/I | Stores Quantity U/I | Dock Quantity U/Ø | RTV Quantity U/Ø | Stores Quantity U/Ø | Inv. System | IAC | Part → No.

USAGE CODES 264 272 280 288 296 304 312 320

Part Number | Part No. Change Letter | Mfg.- No | BPA No | Expiry Date Mo Day Yr | Valid WØ Ind. | Format Ind. | Parent Charge | Prime Contract →

USAGE CODES 328 336 344 352 360 368 376 384

Prime Contract | Seller No. Size Number | Nickname | Small Bus | Type Proc | Action | ASL Use | ATP | P30 Terms | Invoice Terms | FØB VIA | Tag Required | T- Codes 1 2

USAGE CODES 392 400 408 416 424 432 440 448

T - Codes 3 4 5 6 | T60 | T62 | Buyer Group | Buyer Sort | Buyer Grp Sort | Pre Action | U/I | Test Rept. | DMS | Dock | Quality | Packaging | Mat'l Catgy | Weight Conversion Factor | Description 1 → | CHECK (✓) IF RECORD IS CONT

USAGE CODES 456 464 472 480 488 496 504 512

COMMENTS

PREPARED BY | DATE | ESTIMATED RECORD QUANTITY LOW 60,000 HIGH 100,000 | Check (✓) | ORGANIZATION METHOD: SEQUENCE, INDEX SEQUENCE, DIRECT, RELATIVE | USER LABELS: YES, NO | RECORD FORM: FIXED LENGTH, VARIABLE LENGTH, UNDEFINED LENGTH

RECORD LENGTH 650 | BYTES PER BLOCK | SEQUENCE FIELDS, MAJOR TO MINOR (ENTER WHEN MACHINE SEQUENCED) | INPUT TO | OUTPUT FROM

SYSTEM/FILE NAME | RECORD NAME PDA PO Master | COP FILE I.D. | PAGE | OF

Figure 13. 360 Data Record Layout (cont.)

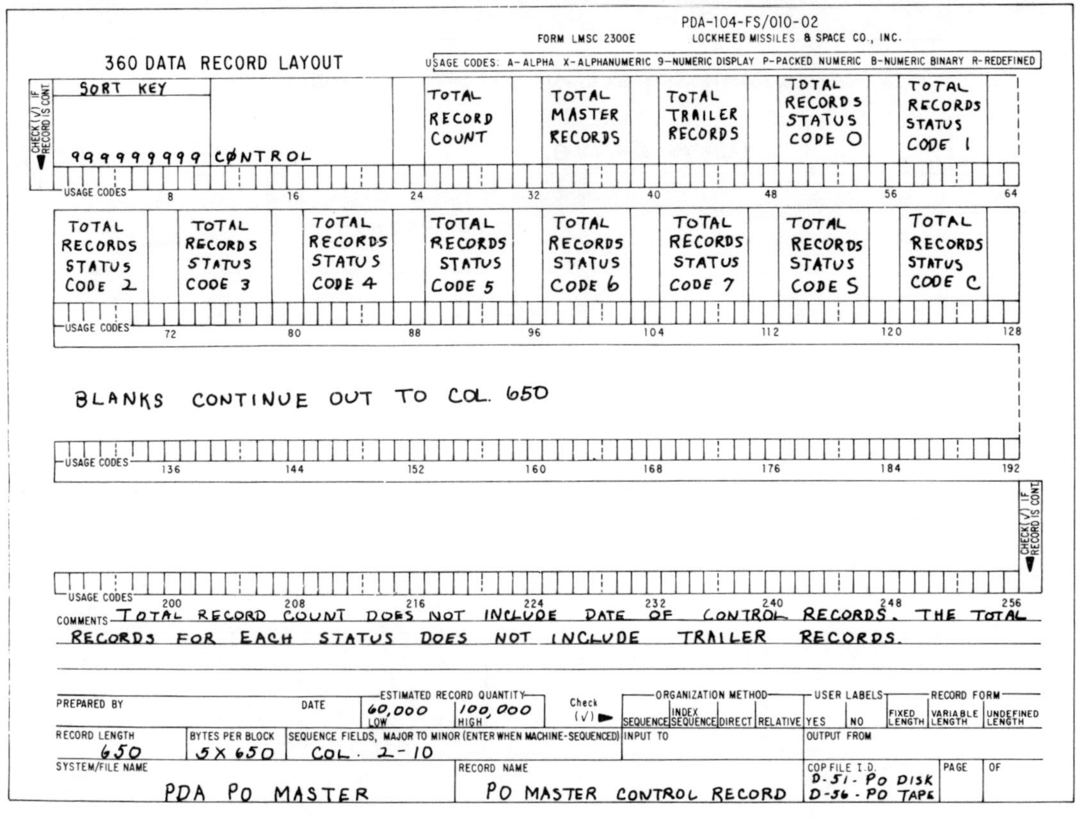

PDA-104-FS/010-02
FORM LMSC 2300E LOCKHEED MISSILES & SPACE CO., INC.

360 DATA RECORD LAYOUT

USAGE CODES: A-ALPHA X-ALPHANUMERIC 9-NUMERIC DISPLAY P-PACKED NUMERIC B-NUMERIC BINARY R-REDEFINED

Columns	Field
1–9	SORT KEY 999999999
10–24	CONTROL
25–32	TOTAL RECORD COUNT
33–40	TOTAL MASTER RECORDS
41–48	TOTAL TRAILER RECORDS
49–56	TOTAL RECORDS STATUS CODE 0
57–64	TOTAL RECORDS STATUS CODE 1
65–72	TOTAL RECORDS STATUS CODE 2
73–80	TOTAL RECORDS STATUS CODE 3
81–88	TOTAL RECORDS STATUS CODE 4
89–96	TOTAL RECORDS STATUS CODE 5
97–104	TOTAL RECORDS STATUS CODE 6
105–112	TOTAL RECORDS STATUS CODE 7
113–120	TOTAL RECORDS STATUS CODE S
121–128	TOTAL RECORDS STATUS CODE C

BLANKS CONTINUE OUT TO COL. 650

COMMENTS: TOTAL RECORD COUNT DOES NOT INCLUDE DATE OF CONTROL RECORDS. THE TOTAL RECORDS FOR EACH STATUS DOES NOT INCLUDE TRAILER RECORDS.

PREPARED BY: | DATE: | ESTIMATED RECORD QUANTITY: LOW 60,000 HIGH 100,000 | Check (√) ORGANIZATION METHOD: SEQUENCE, INDEX SEQUENCE, DIRECT, RELATIVE | USER LABELS: YES, NO | RECORD FORM: FIXED LENGTH, VARIABLE LENGTH, UNDEFINED LENGTH

RECORD LENGTH: 650 | BYTES PER BLOCK: 5 X 650 | SEQUENCE FIELDS, MAJOR TO MINOR (ENTER WHEN MACHINE-SEQUENCED): COL. 2-10 | INPUT TO: | OUTPUT FROM:

SYSTEM/FILE NAME: PDA PO MASTER | RECORD NAME: PO MASTER CONTROL RECORD | COP FILE I.D.: D-51-PO DISK, D-56-PO TAPE | PAGE | OF

Figure 13. 360 Data Record Layout (cont.)

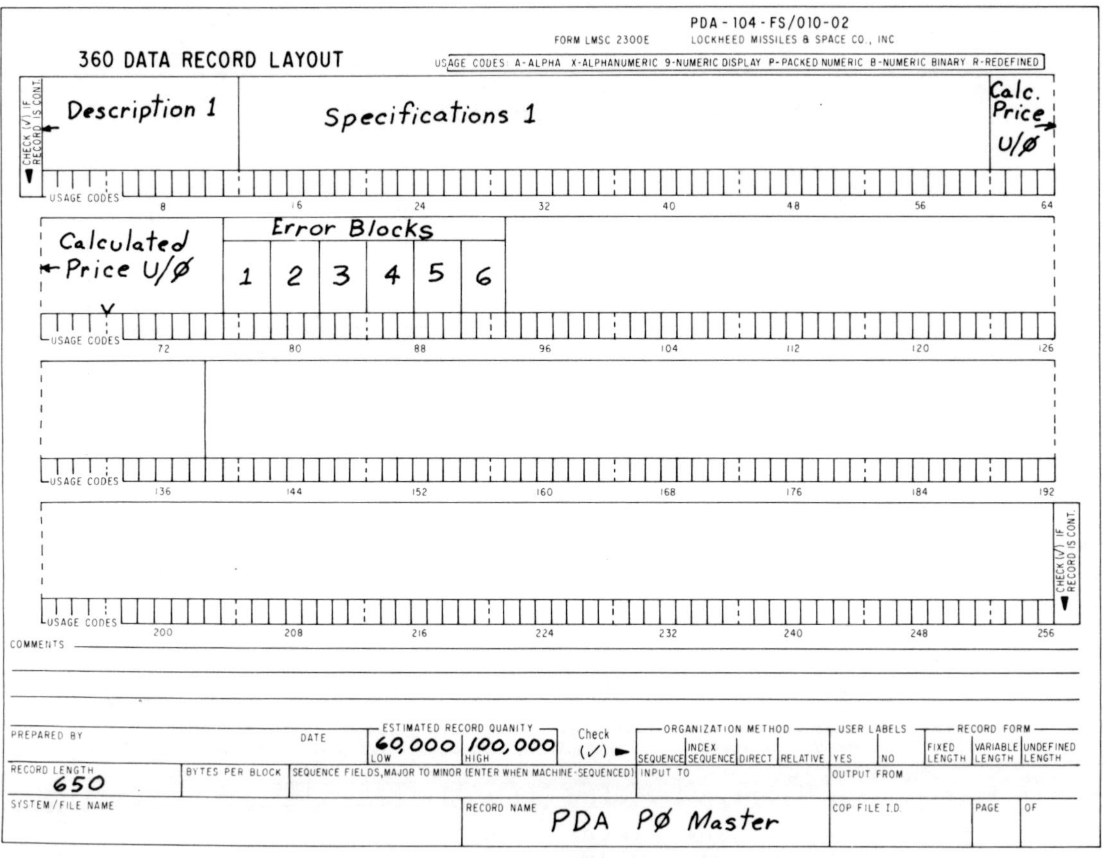

FORM LMSC 2300E

PDA - 104 - FS/010-02

LOCKHEED MISSILES & SPACE CO., INC

360 DATA RECORD LAYOUT

USAGE CODES: A-ALPHA X-ALPHANUMERIC 9-NUMERIC DISPLAY P-PACKED NUMERIC B-NUMERIC BINARY R-REDEFINED

CHECK (✓) IF RECORD IS CONT.

Description 1 | Specifications 1 | Calc. Price U/Ø

USAGE CODES 8 16 24 32 40 48 56 64

Calculated Price U/Ø | Error Blocks 1 2 3 4 5 6

USAGE CODES 72 80 88 96 104 112 120 126

USAGE CODES 136 144 152 160 168 176 184 192

USAGE CODES 200 208 216 224 232 240 248 256

CHECK (✓) IF RECORD IS CONT.

COMMENTS

PREPARED BY | DATE | ESTIMATED RECORD QUANITY: LOW 60,000, HIGH 100,000 | Check (✓) ► | ORGANIZATION METHOD: SEQUENCE, INDEX SEQUENCE, DIRECT, RELATIVE | USER LABELS: YES, NO | RECORD FORM: FIXED LENGTH, VARIABLE LENGTH, UNDEFINED LENGTH

RECORD LENGTH 650 | BYTES PER BLOCK | SEQUENCE FIELDS, MAJOR TO MINOR (ENTER WHEN MACHINE-SEQUENCED) | INPUT TO | OUTPUT FROM

SYSTEM/FILE NAME | RECORD NAME PDA PØ Master | COP FILE I.D. | PAGE | OF

Figure 13. 360 Data Record Layout (cont.)

SAMP

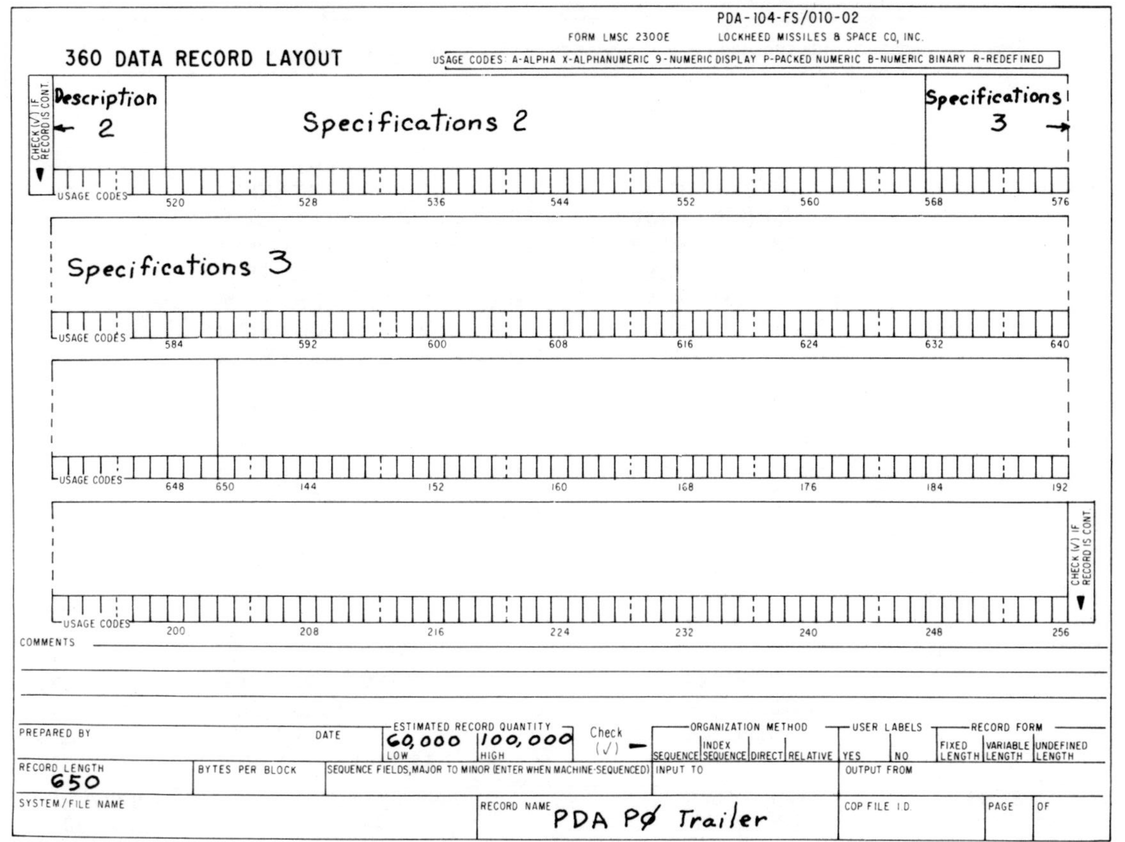

PDA-104-FS/010-02

FORM LMSC 2300E LOCKHEED MISSILES & SPACE CO, INC.

360 DATA RECORD LAYOUT

USAGE CODES: A-ALPHA X-ALPHANUMERIC 9-NUMERIC DISPLAY P-PACKED NUMERIC B-NUMERIC BINARY R-REDEFINED

CHECK (√) IF RECORD IS CONT

Description ← 2

Specifications 2

Specifications 3 →

USAGE CODES 520 528 536 544 552 560 568 576

Specifications 3

USAGE CODES 584 592 600 608 616 624 632 640

USAGE CODES 648 650 144 152 160 168 176 184 192

USAGE CODES 200 208 216 224 232 240 248 256

CHECK (√) IF RECORD IS CONT

COMMENTS

PREPARED BY | DATE | ESTIMATED RECORD QUANTITY LOW 60,000 HIGH 100,000 | Check (√) | ORGANIZATION METHOD: SEQUENCE, INDEX SEQUENCE, DIRECT, RELATIVE | USER LABELS: YES, NO | RECORD FORM: FIXED LENGTH, VARIABLE LENGTH, UNDEFINED LENGTH

RECORD LENGTH 650 | BYTES PER BLOCK | SEQUENCE FIELDS, MAJOR TO MINOR (ENTER WHEN MACHINE-SEQUENCED) | INPUT TO | OUTPUT FROM

SYSTEM/FILE NAME | RECORD NAME PDA PØ Trailer | COP FILE I.D. | PAGE | OF

Figure 13. 360 Data Record Layout (cont.)

PDA-104-FS/020-02
Date
Company/Division

BLOCK NUMBER	BLOCK DATA NAME	PROGRAM DATA NAME	PICTURE	SIZE	4B COLUMN
I50	PASS THROUGH KEY	KEY	XX	2	2
I50	FACILITY	FACILITY	X	1	3
05	REQUESTOR	REQUESTOR	X	1	4
05	PO SERIAL (LAST 3)	SERIAL-3	X(3)	3	7
05	PO SERIAL (FIRST 2)	SERIAL-2	XX	2	9
05	ITEM CODE	ITEM	X	1	10
I51	TRAILER	TRAILER	X	1	11
21A	SHIP TO	SHIP-TO	X(18)	18	29
44	CONFIRMING INITIALS	INITIALS	X(3)	3	32
53	EXTRANEOUS CHARGE CODE 1	EXTRAN-CHARGE-CD1	X(3)	3	35
53A	EXTRANEOUS CHARGE 1	EXTRAN-CHARGE1	S9(5)V99	7	42
53B	EXTRANEOUS CHARGE CODE 2	EXTRAN-CHARGE-CD2	X(3)	3	45
53C	EXTRANEOUS CHARGE 2	EXTRAN-CHARGE2	S9(5)V99	7	52
53D	EXTRANEOUS CHARGE CODE 3	EXTRAN-CHARGE-CD3	X(3)	3	55
53E	EXTRANEOUS CHARGE 3	EXTRAN-CHARGE3	S9(5)V99	7	62
53F	EXTRANEOUS CHARGE CODE 4	EXTRAN-CHARGE-CD4	X(3)	3	65
53G	EXTRANEOUS CHARGE 4	EXTRAN-CHARGE4	S9(5)V99	7	72
53H	EXTRANEOUS CHARGE CODE 5	EXTRAN-CHARGE-CD5	X(3)	3	75
53I	EXTRANEOUS CHARGE 5	EXTRAN-CHARGE5	S9(5)V99	7	82
53J	EXTRANEOUS CHARGE DESCRPT	EXTRAN-CHARGE-DESC	X(22)	22	104
55	ACKNOWLEDGMENT REQUIRED	ACK-REQUIRED	X	1	105
58	PO DISTRIBUTION 1	DISTRIBUTION 1	X(18)	18	123
58A	PO DISTRIBUTION 2	DISTRIBUTION2	X(18)	18	141

Figure 14. PDA Pass Through Data File: Through the courtesy of LMSC.

SAMP

PDA-104-FS/030-02
Date
Company/Division

SAMPLE

FILES	PROGRAMS				
	P01[a]	P02[b]	P03[c]	P04[d]	P05[e]
PDA MAST(-3)	X				
PDA RM(-3)	X				
PDA PASS THROUGH(-3)	X				
PDA MAST AUDIT(-3)	X				
PDA 5A INV(-3)	X				
PDA STMTS UNST	X	X	X	X	
PDA STMTS SORT	X	X	X		
PDA RMRPT	X		X	X	
PDA MARPT	X		X	X	
PDA 5ARPT	X		X	X	
PDA MAST(-1)					X
PDA RM(0)					X
PDA MAST (0)				X	
PDA MAST AUDI(-1)				X	
PDA 5AINV(0)				X	
PDA PASS THROUGH(-1)				X	
PDA 5A INV(-1)				X	
PDA RM(0)				X	
PDA MAST AUDIT(0)				X	

Legend:

[a]P01 A dummy program used to allocate/delete files
[b]P02 SORT Subprogram
[c]P03 PROCESS Subprogram
[d]P04 UPDATE Program
[e]P05 CAPTURE/SORT/EDIT Program

Quick Reference Chart of Files and Programs

PDA-104-FS/030-02
Date
Company/Division

	SEQUENCE			FILE OUTPUT		
File Name	Input	Output	Initiated	Files	Reports	Displays
PDA MASTER	PO PR DR	PO PR DR	Proc. Doc. Control	ACTP	PO/D-D	PO/DS
PDA RM	RM	RM	Material Dock	MASTER	PO/D-D	PO/DS
PASS THROUGH	PO	PO	PO	MASTER		
MASTER AUDIT	PCN PR	PCN PR	Finance Part.	MASTER	W/S	
5A INVENTORY	PDA 4B	PDA 4B	Proc. Doc. Control	MASTER	PO/DS PR/D/W	PO/DS PR/D/W

Figure 15. File Creation Flow Table

PDA-104-FS/040-02
Date
Company/Division

Common Name	Common Abbreviation	COBOL FD Name	DS Name	Copy/Progr. Lib. Name
PDA MASTER	PDA MAST.	MAST	Same	N.A.
PDA RM	PDA RM	RM	”	”
PASS THROUGH DATA	PASS THROUGH	PAT	”	”
MASTER AUDIT	MAST AUDIT	MAD	”	”
5A INVENTORY	5A INV.	5AI	”	”

Figure 16. File Name Reference Table

SAMPLE

PDA-104-FS/050-02
Date
Company/Division

File	Record Name	Common Abbreviation	FD Record Name	Copy/Prog. Lib. Name
PDA MASTER	Purchase Request	PR	Same	N.A.
	Changed Pur. Req.	CPR	"	"
	Purchase Order	PO	"	"
	Delivery Request	DR	"	"
	Requestor	REQ	"	"
	Item Code	IC	"	"
	Trailer Indicator	TI	"	"
PDA RM	Facility	FC	"	"
	Requestor	REQ	"	"
	Purchase Order	PO	"	"
	Item Code	IC	"	"
	RM Number	RMN	"	"
	Split Code	SC	"	"
MASTER AUDIT	Charge Number	CHN	"	"
	Prime Con. Number	PCN	"	"
	Priority Rating	PIR	"	"
	Record Code 09	RC9	"	"
	Work Authority	WA	"	"
	Record Code 05	RC5	"	"
	Project	PRO	"	"
5A INVENTORY	Purchase Request	PR	"	"
	Purchase Order	PO	"	"
	Part Number	PN	"	"
	Item Code	IC	"	"
	Inv. Account No.	IAC	"	"

Figure 17. Record Name Reference Table

SAMP

PDA-104-FS/060-02
Date
Company/Division

SAMPLE

FILE NOMENCLATURE

PDA MASTER	The major file of the system. It contains Purchase Requests, Changed Purchase Requests, Purchase Orders, and Delivery Requests. The file is updated by real-time input and from batch information once a week.
PDA RM	The Receiving Memo File. The input is material received at the dock. When the sum of the quantities received in stores for all of the RMs against one Purchase Order equals the quantity ordered, the Purchase Order is materially closed.
PASS THROUGH DATA	A temporary file that stores "Pass Through" data for a Purchase Order until all of the data for that particular Purchase Order have been corrected. This file consists of 20 records set up permanently, with Sort Keys of 01 through 20.
MASTER AUDIT	Updated by the Finance Partition. It is accessed only by the PDA real-time system to validate Charge Numbers and to pick up Prime Contract Numbers and Priority Ratings.
5A INVENTORY	Updated by PDA 4B when: (1) an inventory PR/PO is added to the PDA 4B Master File, and (2) material is received in stores.

BOOK/SECTION III

PROGRAMMING SPECIFICATIONS

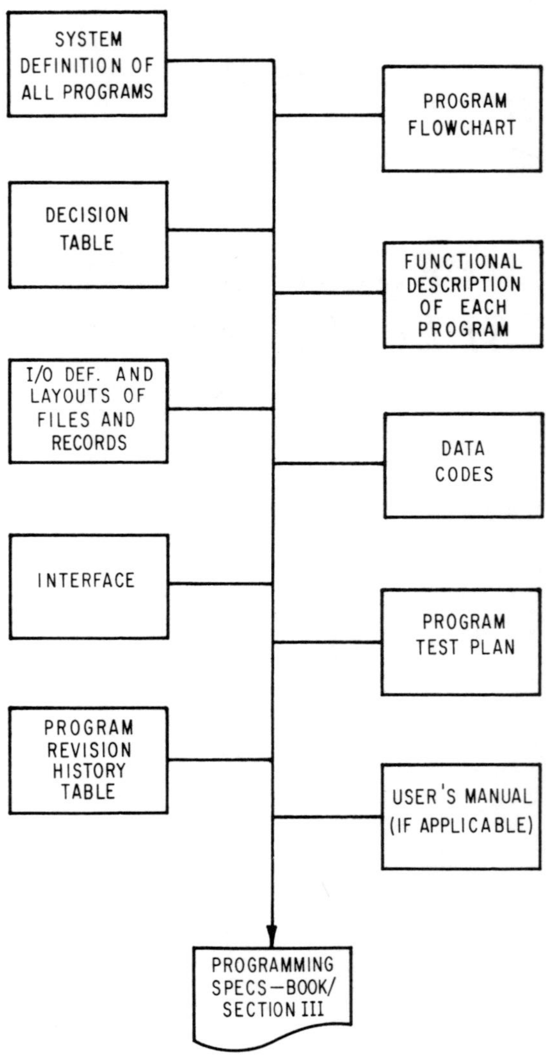

Figure 18. Organization of Book/Section III: Programming Specifications

CONTENTS

PROGRAMMING SPECIFICATIONS (XX-000-PS/000-00)*

This book/section is necessary for the proper maintenance of programs within the system. It describes to the programmer—usually someone other than the original programmer—the program logic and exception conditions so that he can modify, debug, or change the computer programs. Program documentation is also needed by the operations group if they are to provide efficient production runs.

If the system is designed to be handled by personnel other than computer programmers, for example, a sales backlog report system to be run by the marketing department, then in addition to a program specifications book, a user manual should also be provided.

A program specifications book can contain program listings with appropriate comments *or* detailed (macro- or microlevel) flowcharts. One or the other *must* be included, however, so that the programmer can understand the internal organization of the system's programs. If flowcharts are included in the specifications book, the program listings should be available in the data processing library.

SYSTEM DEFINITION OF ALL PROGRAMS (XX-000-PS/010-00)

In this section the programming philosophy and the program's logical structure is described. The section includes identification of the type of application, a general description of the objectives and functions of the programs, and where the objectives and functions fit into the system. If the system specification of a certain program includes an algorithm or unusual programming technique, this should be stated here.

(*Note*: An algorithm may be described as a precisely defined set of rules to solve a specific problem within a finite number of steps. The program flowchart is one of many examples of an algorithm.)

For a quick grasp of logical structure—that is, the interrelationship of conditions and actions against a set of rules—a decision table is a handy medium. (For a sample form of a decision table, see Figure 20.)

*(XX-000-PS/000-00) follows the indexing system described in the Introduction.

PROGRAM FLOWCHARTS (XX-000-PS/020-00)

Unless a highly complex logic is used in the programs, macrolevel programming flowcharts are recommended. At this level the flowchart is sufficiently detailed to give a clear picture of the design and logic of the program, subprogram, or routine. The macrolevel flowchart is more comprehensive than the system flowchart, yet not quite as detailed as the microlevel flowchart.

To be useful, that is, so that someone other than the original programmer can follow the logical structure of the program, a program flowchart should be clearly labeled. Moreover, the coding *must* relate to the program listings and not be overly crowded with details if it is to cross-reference with the program listings. Better yet, the labels of the program listings can become specifics indicating not only symbols but the exact location of that particular routine on the flowchart. For example, the "ST03-D4" ID label on the program listing means "SORT Routine, page 3, grid position D4 on the flowchart."

Note: For effective program maintenance it is imperative that whenever the program logic is modified, the flowcharts, in addition to the files and documentation, be updated also.

It is good practice for the computer facility to establish standard flowcharting symbols and enforce their use, whether hand-drawn flowcharts or automated flowcharts (via a flowcharting program) are used. The following symbols conform to the American National Standards Institute (ANSI) X3.5 flowchart standard symbols.

FUNCTIONAL DESCRIPTION OF EACH PROGRAM (XX-000-PS/030-00)

a. *Background Information* is a narrative description of each program within the system elaborated by detailed statement of the algorithm. The program's ID name and assigned number, as well as the program's purpose and function(s), are given. Also, the program logic within the functions (perhaps in a logic flow table), the options, and any special programming technique used are described. A decision table such as Figure 20 is helpful in defining the problem. If necessary, combine certain problems by analyzing the required order of input and output data, and thus–through relating the cause (conditions) to the effect (actions)–show the program logic. The calling sequence of subprograms (modules) that carry out the functions of the program is included. Program modifications are also described here–that is, if the program is modified, what to look for; if

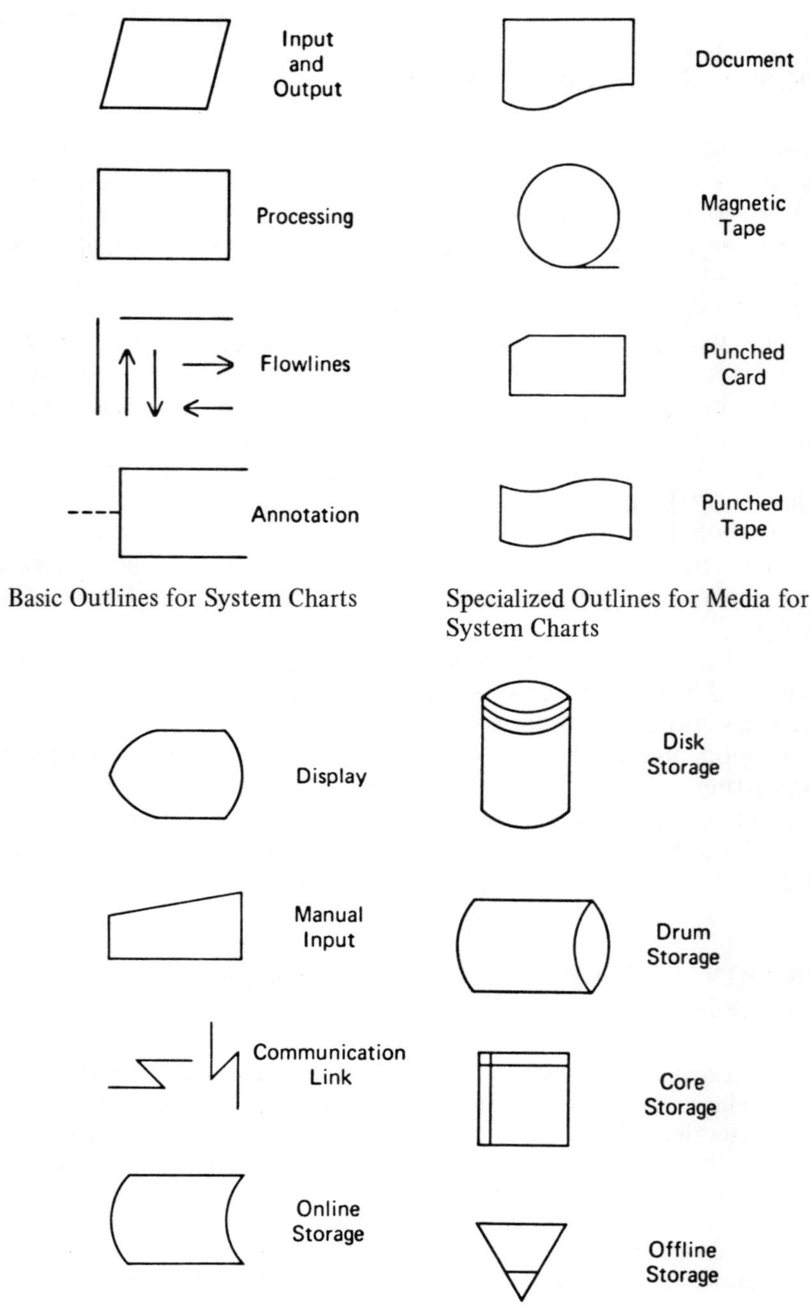

Basic Outlines for System Charts

Specialized Outlines for Media for System Charts

Specialized Outlines for Equipment for System Charts

Figure 19. Standard Flowcharting Symbols. From Ned Chapin, *Flowcharts,* Auerbach Publishers, Princeton, N.J., 1971, pp. 45, 48, 50.

there are exceptions (other than normal processing) within the program, what they are and so forth.

b. *Frequency* states how often the program is being run to produce the desired output.

c. *Hardware Configuration* lists the minimum hardware—for example, "The system is designed for PDP-9, 16K, Console Teletype (KSR33 or KSR35), paper tape reader and punch, 2 magnetic tapes, 1 disk, and 1 line printer."

d. *Software Configuration* states what language the program is using for a particular application—for example, COBOL for an inventory control system program; Assembly Language for a heavily used, large, extended tape/disk storage system program, and so on. Also, utility programs are described (subroutine library, square root routine, plotting routine, data formating routine).

e. *Operating System* states the type (OS, DOS, MCP, etc.) for which the program is designed.

f. *Files.* For details on the file and I/O, see Book/Section II, File and I/O Specifications. If specific information about the files is required here, the modular matrix chart—showing names, input/output, sequence, etc., from Figure 15 of the FS Sample Application—may be inserted.

g. *Data Element Reference Table* is a tabular form showing the data elements that make up the program. (See Figure 9 for sample form.)

h. *Reference Chart of Programs and Files* is a table that cross-references files with the programs that use those tables. (It is also a modular table. For sample form, see Figure 15 of Sample Application, File Specifications.)

i. *Coding and Labeling* is an explanation of the coded instructions in the program listing. This encourages uniform format and better coding quality. Quality coding and meaningful program labels make for readily understood program listings, and consequently, better program maintenance.

j. *Control* sets up criteria for certain conditions such as error tolerances, checkpoints for error recovery, and control files created by the program.

k. *Miscellaneous Instruction* includes any additional information not covered in category j.

DATA CODES (XX-000-PS/040-00)

A definition of the transaction codes (T/C) for input and a description of their functions makes the maintenance programmer's task easier.

a. *Definition* is an explanation of what each data code within the program is, for example, "Line Item (T/C: 101 = Delete; 102 = Add; 103 = Change)."

b. *Index* is a list of codes used.

c. *Assigned Data Codes and Their Meaning* is a description of the type of codes and their meaning. Examples are: (1) "Marketing Number–Sequential Number assigned by Marketing, corresponding to a customer specification" and (2) "Job Order Number–The number used to collect all costs associated with that line item." The description also gives the range of legal and illegal codes.

d. *Code Structure* is a description of the range of allowable values, the number (or symbol) base used, as well as the method to calculate which code to select for various data and the characteristics of these codes.

INTERFACE (XX-000-PS/050-00)

This section cites and describes the interaction of subprograms (modules), routines, files, records, and macros that communicate with or are used by the documented program and other programs of other systems. For example, "PROCESS program receives control after SORT has decided the function to be executed, that is, Inproof, Sort, or Resort. These programs receive control and pass items to the program that creates the CONTROL and EDIT data sets."

PROGRAM TEST PLAN (XX-000-PS/060-00)

Before preparing a test plan that is a methodical sequence of test operations, it is advisable to check the program against the flowchart, as well as keypunch errors by the flags in the program, so that in case of incorrect reference or instruction, it can be corrected before going into lengthy and expensive debugging.

Once this is done, it should be determined what type of testing will be done and the method of doing it; that is, whether the main logic of the program will be affected–for example, to delete from or insert a record into the master file, and to run the test by running the program parallel with live data, or to use a "testing program." To use a testing program means using a special program consisting of artificial data designed to run the system program through a series of operations, testing some or all of its phases.

Because testing is not a one-time operation (it has to be done not only for debugging the original program but every time the program has to be revised), the tests should be documented. It is important that the test plan bear the date, time, and program(s) affected. Moreover, if a debugged program is revised, the original version of the program should be kept in the data processing library for a certain period of time for possible reference.

The test documentation, in short, should state the inputs, test procedures, sample run showing I/O, console log, and the outputs or results.

PROGRAM REVISIONS (XX-000-PS/070-00)

A history of all revisions—from requests to distribution—is recorded here via a standard form, so that all affected personnel are kept abreast of program changes. The sample form (Figure 21) is self-explanatory.

USER'S MANUAL (IF APPLICABLE) (XX-000-PS/080-00)*

If the programs in the system are designed for and manipulated by personnel other than EDP personnel, such as a department outside the data processing group, a separate user's manual should be provided.

This manual should consist of the following sections:

a. *General System* is a general description or overview of the system and the programs within the system, its objectives, and data flow.
b. *System Flowchart* is a clearly coded and labeled flowchart with appropriate comments and short explanatory notes.
c. *Input Description* is an explanation of what the user must provide to receive the desired output. He has to know the transaction codes, what types of codes the program accepts, the program options, and how the program is updated. It clarifies the error and exception statements for the user, as well as the action to be taken.
d. *Output Description* is an explanation of the reports, messages on the console terminal, or the visual output on the CRT display system if it's an on-line, time sharing system.

*This section is a separate entity and not part of the Programming Specification section, since User's Manual may have a separate distribution. It is included here for the sake of economy and because the programmer usually supervises the preparation of the User's Manual.

e. *Procedure Description* is a set of instructions on how to input data, the input forms, and any special procedures, for example, "If the change order is a *change* to an existing item on the file, use the same item number. If it is an *addition* to the Sales Order, give the next item number in sequence."

f. *Operations Instructions* is a detailed description of procedures, that is, operation requirements, error messages, restarts, job control, and so on.

g. *Glossary* is an essential part of the user's manual. It clarifies EDP terminology (both general and unique to the facility) to personnel not acquainted with data processing language.

SYSTEM/PROGRAM NAME: SYSTEM/PROGRAM NUMBER:													DATE:			
CONDITION STUB	**RULES**															
	1	**2**	**3**	**4**	**5**	**6**	**7**	**8**	**9**	**10**	**11**	**12**	**13**	**14**	**15**	**16**
Account Status	Y	Y	Y	Y	Y	Y	Y	Y	N	N	N	N	N	N	N	N
Pay History	Y	Y	N	N	Y	Y	N	N	Y	Y	N	N	Y	Y	N	N
Order Limit	Y	N	Y	N	Y	N	Y	N	Y	N	Y	N	Y	N	Y	N
ACTION STUB																
Process Order	X		X		X		X		X		X		X		X	
Check Order	X		X		X		X		X		X		X		X	
Hold Up Order	X		X		X		X		X		X		X		X	

Legend: Y = true; N = false; X = action

Figure 20. Decision Table (XX-000-PS/010-00)

ITEM	COMMENTS	DATE	REVISED BY
System Name & Number:			
Program Name & Number:			
Requestor: (authorized by:)			
Reason For Revision:			
Target Date for Completion:			
Programmer Responsible:			
Necessary Action:			
Input/Output Formats:			
Flowchart Diagram:			
Program Listing:			
Run Frequency:			
Distribution (to the affected personnel):			

Figure 21. Program Revision History (XX-000-PS/080-00)

LB-101-PS/000-00*
Date
Company/Division

SAMPLE APPLICATION:

ACM LABEL PROGRAM—PROGRAM SPECIFICATIONS

*For the index key, please see the Introduction.

CONTENTS

LB-101-PS/000-00
Date
Company/Division

SAMPLE

Program No. & Name: LB-101, ACM LABEL PROGRAM Date:

Programming Group Leader: (Name) Computer Programmer: (Name)

Items required and contained in this book/section	Yes	No	Comments (if no is checked)
1. System Definition of the Program	✓		
2. Decision Table		✓	N.A. This simple program does not require a Decision Table.
3. Program Flowchart	✓		
4. Functional Description of the Program	✓		
5. I/O Definition, Layouts of Files & Records		✓	See Program Listing
6. Data Codes		✓	See Program listing
7. Interface		✓	N.A. Reason same as in No. 2.
8. Program Test Plan		✓	N.A. " " " " " "
9. Program Revision		✓	N.A. " " " " " "
10. User's Manual	✓		

Figure 22. Documentation Checklist

LB-101-PS/000-00
Date
Company/Division

PROGRAM SPECIFICATIONS

While the Book/Section III directive is a guideline for large and medium systems with many computer programs interfacing, in the case of a simple, stand-alone program, a clearly labeled program flowchart and a program listing with a very brief narrative description are sufficient. The important factor is that the program is documented in the standard form and available in a binder for the maintenance programmer. A simple program has been chosen as the sample application to illustrate this point.

SYSTEM DEFINITION OF ALL PROGRAMS—LB-101-PS/010-00

Since the ACM LABEL program is a stand-alone program, it is not a part of any system. Moreover, it has only one purpose, to print the members' address labels for the San Francisco ACM (Association for Computing Machinery) Bay Area Chapters.

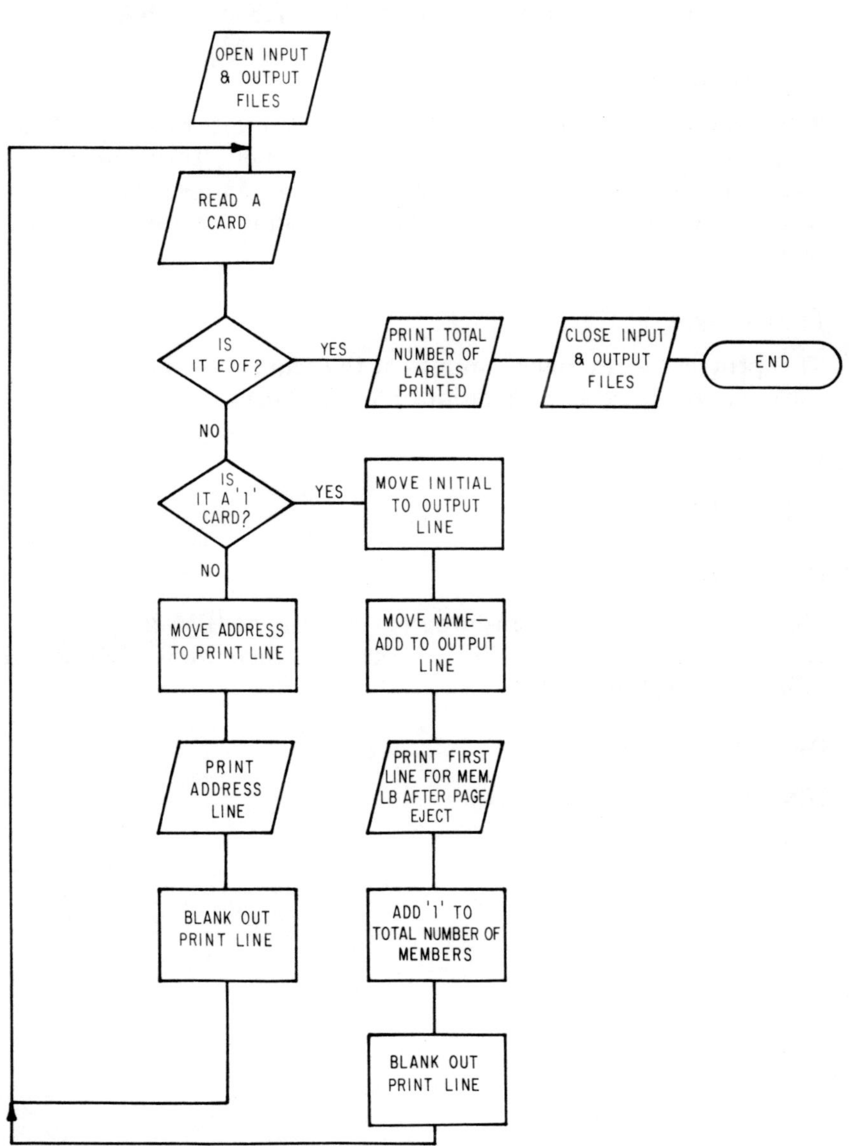

Figure 23. Program Flowchart

LB-101-PS/030-00
Date
Company/Division

FUNCTIONAL DESCRIPTION OF THE PROGRAM

a. Background Information

The program's ID name is LABELS, and its number is 1138. The purpose of the program is to print address labels. The input consists of punched cards containing names and addresses of the local ACM members. Column number 1 is an identifier of another member.

b. Frequency

This program is run once a month at the request of the editor of the chapter's official publication, *The Bit Dropper*.

c. Language

ANS COBOL.

d. Configuration

Minimum hardware for this program consists of IBM 360/50, 1 Disk Drive, shared Model 65 II, 1 reacher punch, model 2540, and 1 line printer, Model 1403.

e. Operating System

IBM Operating System (OS).

```
LEVEL  1OCT69                                              OS USAS COBOL

   1

         01   IDENTIFICATION DIVISION.
         02   PROGRAM-ID. LABELS.
         03   AUTHOR.      JUDITH M. GOLUB.
         04   DATE-WRITTEN.   JUNE 1970.
         05   ENVIRONMENT DIVISION.
         06   CONFIGURATION SECTION.
         07   SOURCE-COMPUTER.    IBM-360-F30.
         08   OBJECT-COMPUTER.    IBM-360-F30.
         09   INPUT-OUTPUT SECTION.
         10   FILE-CONTROL.
         11       SELECT CARD ASSIGN TO UR-2540R-S-SYS032.
    **   11       SELECT PRINTER ASSIGN TO UR-1403-S-SYS034.
         13   DATA DIVISION.
         14   FILE SECTION.
         15   FD  CARD
                  LABEL RECORDS ARE OMITTED
                  RECORDING MODE IS F
         16       RECORD CONTAINS 80 CHARACTERS
         18       DATA RECORD IS ACM-MEM.
         20   01  ACM-MEM SYNC.
         21       02  CARD-NO                         PICTURE X(1).
         22       02  FILLER                          PICTURE X(3).
         23       02  NAME-ADD                        PICTURE X(36).
                      02  INITIAL                     PICTURE X(6).
                      02  FILLER                      PICTURE X(4).
         24       02  ZIP                             PICTURE X(5).
    **   01       02  MEM-NO                          PICTURE X(4).
         02       02  FILLER                          PICTURE X(1).
         03       02  CO-CODE                         PICTURE X(3).
         04       02  FILLER                          PICTURE X(9).
         05       02  NEW-RE                          PICTURE X(3).
         06       02  FILLER                          PICTURE X(5).
              FD  PRINTER
                  RECORDING MODE IS F
                  LABEL RECORDS ARE OMITTED
                  RECORD CONTAINS 36 CHARACTERS
                  DATA RECORD  IS MEM-LIST.
              01  MEM-LIST                            PICTURE X(36) SYNC.
         09   WORKING-STORAGE SECTION.
         11   77  LIMT          COMPUTATIONAL         PICTURE S9999 VALUE ZEROS
                                                                           SYNC.
    **   10   01  PRINT-LINE SYNC.
         11       03  LINE-NAME.
                      05  FILLER                      PICTURE XX VALUE SPACES.
                      05  INITIAL                     PICTURE X(3).
                      05  FILLER                      PICTURE X(1)    VALUE SPACE.
         13           05  NAME-ADD                    PICTURE X(30).
                  03  LINE-ADD REDEFINES LINE-NAME.
                      05  FILLER                      PICTURE XX.
                      05  NAME-ADD                    PICTURE X(34).
    **   06   PROCEDURE DIVISION.
         08   OPEN-RTN.
         09       OPEN INPUT CARD.
                  OPEN OUTPUT PRINTER.
```

Figure 24. ANS COBOL. Through the courtesy of Singer-Link Data Center.

2

```
        10  READ-REC.
        11      READ CARD AT END GO TO END-RTN.
        12      IF CARD-NO = 1 GO TO  FIRST-CARD.
**      02  SAME-MEM.
                MOVE NAME-ADD OF ACM-MEM TO NAME-ADD OF LINE-ADD.
                WRITE MEM-LIST FROM PRINT-LINE AFTER POSITIONING 1 LINES.
                MOVE SPACES TO PRINT-LINE.
        10      GO TO READ-REC.
        15  FIRST-CARD.
                MOVE INITIAL OF ACM-MEM TO INITIAL OF LINE-NAME.
        18      MOVE NAME-ADD OF ACM-MEM TO NAME-ADD OF LINE-NAME.
                WRITE MEM-LIST FROM PRINT-LINE AFTER POSITIONING 0 LINES.
**      04      ADD 1 TO LIMT.
                MOVE SPACES TO PRINT-LINE.
                GO TO READ-REC.
        12  END-RTN.
                DISPLAY LIMT.
        13      CLOSE CARD.
                CLOSE PRINTER.
        14      GOBACK.
```

Figure 24. ANS COBOL (cont.)

SOC-106-PS/080-00*
Date
Company/Division

SAMPLE APPLICATION:

SALES ORDER CONTROL SYSTEM—USER'S MANUAL

*For the index key, please see the Introduction.

SOC-106-PS/080-00
Date
Company/Division

SAMP

Contents

SOC-106-PS/080-00
Date
Company/Division

SAMPLE

System No. & Name: SOC-106, SALES ORDER CONTROL SYSTEM Date:

Responsible Marketing Department Personnel: (Name)

Items required and contained in this book/section	Yes	No	Comments (if no is checked)
1. General System	✓		
2. System Flowchart	✓		
3. Input Description	✓		
4. Output Description	✓		
5. Procedure Description	✓		
6. Clerical Procedures	✓		
7. Operations Instructions	✓		
8. Input Form Item Record	✓		
9. Input Form Data Record	✓		
10. Glossary	✓		

Figure 25. Documentation Checklist

SOC-106-PS/090-00
Date
Company/Division

GENERAL SYSTEM

The sales order control system was designed to control the company's sales orders. It is run daily to maintain an up-to-date sales order file and produce daily reports.

a. Hardware Configuration: Burroughs B5500. The system uses 15K for its programs, the Burroughs fixed-head disk system, the Burroughs printer, card reader, and punch.
b. Software Configuration: The system runs under Disk File Master Control Program (DF MCP) and uses COBOL Language, F level.
c. Estimate of Running Time: Approximately 10 minutes.
d. Programs: The sales order control (SOC) consists of three programs: SORT, EDIT (input); UPDATE; and REPORT GENERATOR. The sequence of execution and file handling is controlled by the programmed flow of operations. Detailed listing and error-listing reports are generated by the SORT, EDIT program during data input. The UPDATE program updates the sales order backlog file by device/sales order/item number.
e. Files: All files are sequential.
f. Reports: Reports generated by SOC are: (1) Device/Sales Backlog Status (daily), (2) Backlog Summary (weekly), (3) Period Sales/Backlog Status (on request), and (4) Sales Order Master File (on request).

Zero Backing Reports, Schedule/Order Reports, Schedule Date Reports, and Backlog Compare Reports are generated as Exception Reports.

SAMPLE

This procedure (chaining of programs processing, or "ZIP" from one program to the next) is possible on the Burroughs System.

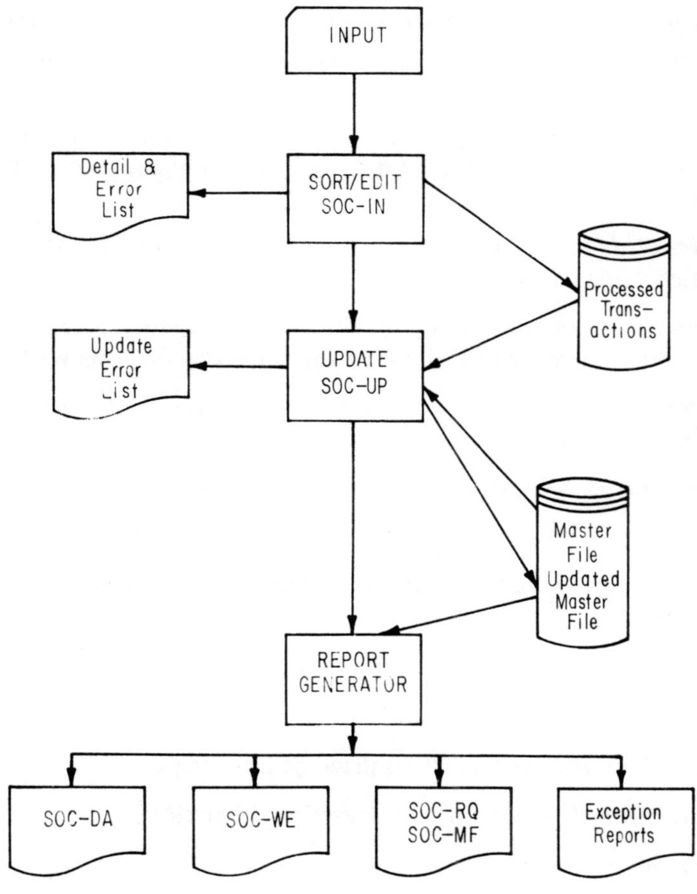

Figure 26. System Flowchart

SOC-106-PS/110-00
Date
Company/Division

INPUT DESCRIPTION

All inputs must have as a minimum: (1) a transaction code (T/C) and (2) control information (device number, sales order number, and item number). The SORT, EDIT program accepts four different types of records.

a. Line Item (T/C: 101 = delete, 102 = add, 103 = change)

This record is maintained by the Marketing department (MD) from their copy of the sales order and contains the following information:

1. *Device Number.* The part number that is on the device; also used as the basic number for all documentation in support of that device.
2. *Sales Order Number.* Sequential number assigned by Marketing which appears on all sales orders.
3. *Item.* Number that identifies the items on the sales order; generally predetermined by the way the purchase order is written.
4. *Job Order Number.* The number used to collect all costs associated with that line item.
5. *Description.* Description of device or line item.
6. *Customer.* Self-explanatory.
7. *Blanket Order.* Self-explanatory. They are identified by a "B" in this field.
8. *Unit of Measure.* E = Each; L = Lot; S = Set.
9. *Unit Price.* Price of one unit.
10. *Sales Amount.* Total selling price of line item.
11. *Order Quantity.* Quantity released and backlogged.
12. *Change Order Number.*

b. Original Scheduled Delivery (T/C: 104 = delete, 105 = add)

This record is maintained by MD and contains the original date and quantity scheduled by Production Control. Multiple entries result if Production Control schedules partial shipments.

SOC-106-PS/110-00
Date
Company/Division

SAMPLE

1. *Date.* Original scheduled date.

2. *QTY.* Quantity scheduled for shipment.

3. *CG.* Change order number.

c. **Scheduled Delivery (T/C: 106 = delete, 107 = add)**

This record is maintained by Production Control and is the date and quantity the Production Department is committed to. There are multiple entries if partial shipments are scheduled.

1. *Date.* Scheduled delivery date.

2. *QTY.* Scheduled delivery quantity.

3. *CG.* Change order number.

d. **Actual Deliveries (T/C: 108 = delete, 109 = add)**

This record is maintained by Production Control and is a record of the actual shipment. It contains quantity shipped, date shipped, actual shipper backlog, and a two-position change number that can be used to indicate the latest Sales Order change number against which the device was shipped.

1. *Date.* Actual delivery date.

2. *QTY.* Actual shipped quantity.

3. *CG.* Change order number.

4. *Backlog.* Actual shipper backlog quantity.

e. **Program Options**

1. *Closures.* A line item and all associated date records can be closed on the file by submitting a line item change card (transaction code 103) with the letter "C" coded in column 79. All closures stay on the file but are not printed on the Device Sales Order Backlog Status Report. The date records cannot be deleted if the line item is in a closed status.

SOC-106-PS/120-00
Date
Company/Division

OUTPUT DESCRIPTION

There are four major reports generated, plus an additional six exception reports. The purpose of these reports is to maintain status on all sales orders.

a. Device/Sales Status Report—SOC-DA

This report is generated daily and lists all open sales orders. The first line for each control (device/sales order/item) is the sales order line item; it contains the fields described in Method of Operation. Next is a listing of all of the original schedule dates and quantities, followed by the scheduled dates and quantities.

The last set of dates for any given control is the date and quantity of each shipment. The program totals all shipments for each control and calculates the total dollar value of those parts shipped as well as the backlog. The program gives similar totals for each type of device.

b. Shipped Summary—SOC-WE

Generated weekly, this report is a summary of the quantity and dollars ordered, shipped, and backlogged for each open sales order line item. The report is in four sequences, as follows:

SOC 1W	Sales Order sequence
SOC 2W	Customer sequence
SOC 3W	Device Number sequence
SOC 4W	Product Line sequence

Each report gives a final total for sales amount, order quantity, quantity shipped, dollars shipped, quantity backlog, and dollar backlog.

c. Period/Sales/Backlog Status Report—SOC-RQ

This report is run at the request of MD and is a summary of shipments for a given period of time.

There is a control card following the execute card that allows the user to control the time span and sequence of the report, as well as the product line reported on. The format for the control is as follows:

SOC-106-PS/120-00
Date
Company/Division

COL	*DESCRIPTION*
1-3	Transaction code is 100
4-9	From date—first date included in the report
10-15	Through date—last date included in the report
16	Product line
17	Sequence

A report of each week's shipments is generated as soon as MD determines that the prior week's data is logged in correctly. Similarly, a monthly report is produced.

d. Sales Order Master File—SOC-MF

This report is identical to SOC-D, except that all records, including those that are closed, are included. The report is generated at the request of MD, about once a month.

e. Exception Reports

1. *Detail Listing.* A listing of all transactions made each day.
2. *Error Listing.* A listing of each day's invalid transactions.
3. *Zero Backlog Listing.* A listing of all line items for which no backlog exists. Change cards (T/C 103) are generated for each of these line items, with a "C" in column 79.
4. *Schedule/Order Quantity Compare Report.* A listing of all line items for which the schedule quantity does not equal the backlog.
5. *Schedule Date Report.* A list in schedule date sequence of all devices scheduled. This report can be used to forecast sales, shipments, and material requirements.
6. *Backlog Compare Report.* A list of all line items for which the backlog as calculated by the program does not agree with the backlog as noted on the shipper.

SOC-106-PS/130-00
Date
Company/Division

PROCEDURE DESCRIPTION

To post and report information correctly and for system control, the following is mandatory.

The two areas where item numbers could be duplicated and the solution to avoid the duplication are:

a. Change Order

1. If the change order is a *change* to an existing item on the file, use the same item number.
2. If it is an *addition* to the Sales Order, give the next item number in sequence.

b. Blanket Order

1. If item to be set up is a Blanket Order, use original item number.
2. On each *Release* for that item, use original item number; also suffix the item number with an alpha character, for example, 1st Release, suffix with "A", 2nd Release, suffix with "B", 3rd Release, suffix with "C", and so on.

Since the system has to postdate records to a specific item number record, it is *essential* that all *Date Record Entries* have the same Sales Order Number, Item Number, and Device Number as the Item Record.

To avoid inflated dollar and backlog totals on all system-generated reports, the following should be noted:

3. *Blanket Orders*

System will not:
—accept unit price
—accept sales amount
—compute backlog
—show order quantity in any totals

All Blanket Orders are indicated by a "B" under column heading (B/O) on all reports.

SOC-106-PS/180-00
Date
Company/Division

SAMPLE

c. Lot Charges (Nonrecurring)

If there is *no* unit price, the system will not compute shipped dollars for that item. Anyone wanting total shipped dollars to date will have to take into account any lot charges with no unit price. Lot charges can be identified on all reports by a "L" under the column heading "UM".

d. Input Forms

Input forms required for this system are:

1. Sales Order Item Record (Form #10)
2. Date and Quantity Record (Form #11)

The following sales order item record entries are required on Form #10:

1. Transaction code
   Use 103 to set up an item record.
   Use 101 to delete an item record.
   Use 102 to change an existing item record.
2. Sales Order No.
3. Item No.
4. Device No.
5. Mkt. No.
6. Quantity ordered.
7. Customer Name
8. Change No. Required only when transaction is reflected by a Change Order. Use change order number as shown on sales order.
9. Description.
10. Job Order No.
11. Unit Price.
12. Amount (Dollar amount of that item).
13. BL/ORD (Blanket Order). Required *only* if item being set up is a blanket order. Enter "B" in this space.

SOC-106-PS/180-00
Date
Company/Division

14. OPN/CLOSE. Enter "Ø if status is to be reported, "C" if status is not to be reported.

15. U.M. (unit of measure). Enter "E" for each, Enter "L" for Lot, Enter "B" for Batch, etc.

To Prepare Date and Quantity Records Entries, fill out Form #11. This multipurpose form can set up and delete three types of records:

1. Original Scheduled Date Record (customer required date).

2. Scheduled Ship Date Record.

3. Actual Ship Date Record.

To prepare date and quantity record entries.

1. Transaction code
   - 104 To Delete original scheduled date record.
   - 105 To set up original scheduled date record.
   - 106 To delete scheduled ship date record.
   - 107 To set up scheduled ship date record.
   - 108 To delete actual ship date record.
   - 109 To set up actual ship date record.

2. Sales Order No.

3. Item No.

4. Device no.

5. Date.

6. Quantity

7. Change no. Required only when transaction is reflected by a change order. Use change order number as shown on sales order.

8. Shipper backlog. Required only on 109 transaction. Enter production controls backlog.

SOC-106-PS/140-00
Date
Company/Division

Item Record Transaction Codes
101 = Delete
102 = Setup
103 = Change

Form No. 10

Transaction Code	Sales Order No.	Item No.	Device No.	Market No.	Quantity Ordered	Customer Name	Change No.	Description	Job Order No.	Unit Price	Amount
1 3	4 8	9 11	12 18	20 25	26 32	33 43	44	46 55	56 63	64 69	70
102	67215	820	5203400	1545	5000	"C" Tool		Screws	65	0003	15000

Figure 27. Sales Order Control Input Item Record

SOC-106-PS/150-00
Date
Company/Division

Data Record Transaction Codes
104 = Delete
105 = Setup
106 = Delete (Scheduled Ship Record)
107 = Change
Actual shipping record 108 = delete
109 = setup

Form No. 11

Transaction Code	Sales Order No.	Item No.	Device No.	Date	Quantity	Change No.	Shipping Backlog	Comments
1 3	4 8	9 11	12 18	19 24	25 30	31 32	33 38	39 70
104	1572	48	580	2/19/71	100		108	Customer cancelled item 2/15/71

Figure 28. Sales Order Control Input Data Record

SOC-106-PS/160-00
Date
Company/Division

CLERICAL PROCEDURES

a. Special Keypunch Instructions

The Master File update cards will be keypunched and verified on the swing shift and submitted to be run into SOC-IN on a daily basis.

b. Retention Periods

1. The Master file is to be retained for five days.
2. All report files are to be scratched as soon as the report is printed.

c. Disposition of Inputs/Outputs

1. All keypunch forms are to be returned to the Marketing department as soon as the file has been updated
2. Detail cards are retained by operations for two weeks.
3. All reports are to be submitted to marketing department for distribution.

d. Processing Schedule

1. *Input.* All transactions are to be coded and turned into keypunch at the end of the day shift.
2. The Master File will be updated daily and reports ready for distribution by 8:00 a.m.

SOC-106-PS/170-00
Date
Company/Division

SAM

OPERATIONS INSTRUCTIONS

a. SOC Programs

Sales Order Control System consists of three programs:

1. SOC-IN Sort and Edit
2. SOC-UP Update
3. SOC-DA/SOC-WE Daily Report Generator/Weekly Report Generator

b. System Flow

1. SOC-IN ZIPS SOC-UP
2. SOC-UP ZIPS SOC-DA
3. SOC-DA ZIPS SOC-WE
4. SOC-WE* ZIPS Library Dump

c. Operation Requirements

1. Pick up cards from keypunch.
2. Insert behind data card (DATA SOC-INB).
3. Execute SOC-IN.
4. Put 5-part paper in printer when SPO asks for it.
5. Label output tape SOCTIL and use it to store Library Maint. Dump. A tape is reversed for each day of the week.
6. Store detail cards by date.
7. Retain execute deck for next day's run.
8. Five tapes are reserved and stored with the permanent library tapes. These tapes are used only for SOCTIL library dumps. These are stored by date, latest date—first tape left, oldest date—last tape right. They are rotated daily. The oldest date then becomes the latest dump tape.

*SOC-WE tests (computer-date) to determine if weekly reports are due; if not, "SPO" message, "No Weekly Reports Today," will appear.

SOC-106-PS/180-00
Date
Company/Division

SAMPLE

d. System Error Messages

Self-explanatory.

e. Restart Procedure

1. Load SOC-UP and SOC-WE from latest SOCTIL tape. (Your log book will tell you which is the latest tape.)
2. Reexecute SOC-IN.

f. Reports (Daily)

1. Monday—5 part, SOC-WE printed, REMOVV = PURGED.
2. Tuesday—10-part, all reports.
3. Wednesday thru Friday—5-part, all reports.

g. Reports (Weekly)

1. First Monday of every month (only).
2. 5-part, all reports.

SOC-106-PS/170-00
Date
Company/Division

SAM

GLOSSARY

access time. The amount of time required for a computer to locate and transfer data from a storage device and have it available for processing.

address. An identification represented by a name, label, or number for a register, location in storage, or any other data source.

COBOL. Common Business Oriented Language. A commercial (business) data processing language.

code. The preparation of problems in computer language for subsequent representation of data, which then is translated into machine language by the computer.

file. A collection of related records treated as a unit, for example, a sequence of records on magnetic tape terminated by an end-of-file mark or a file gap.

label. A key consisting of one or more characters used to identify a body of data (statement or item) in the computer program.

record. A collection of related data elements, items, or codes treated as a unit.

source program. The computer program written in problem-oriented language (COBOL, PL/I, etc.) or procedure-oriented language (FORTRAN, etc.), which is then translated into machine language by the computer.

time sharing. The use of a device for two or more processes by interleaving parts of each process during the same overall time interval.

transaction codes. Numbers used to identify the nature or type of item. For example, the transaction code tells the computer whether the item should be added, changed, or deleted.

BOOK/SECTION IV

CLERICAL PROCEDURES

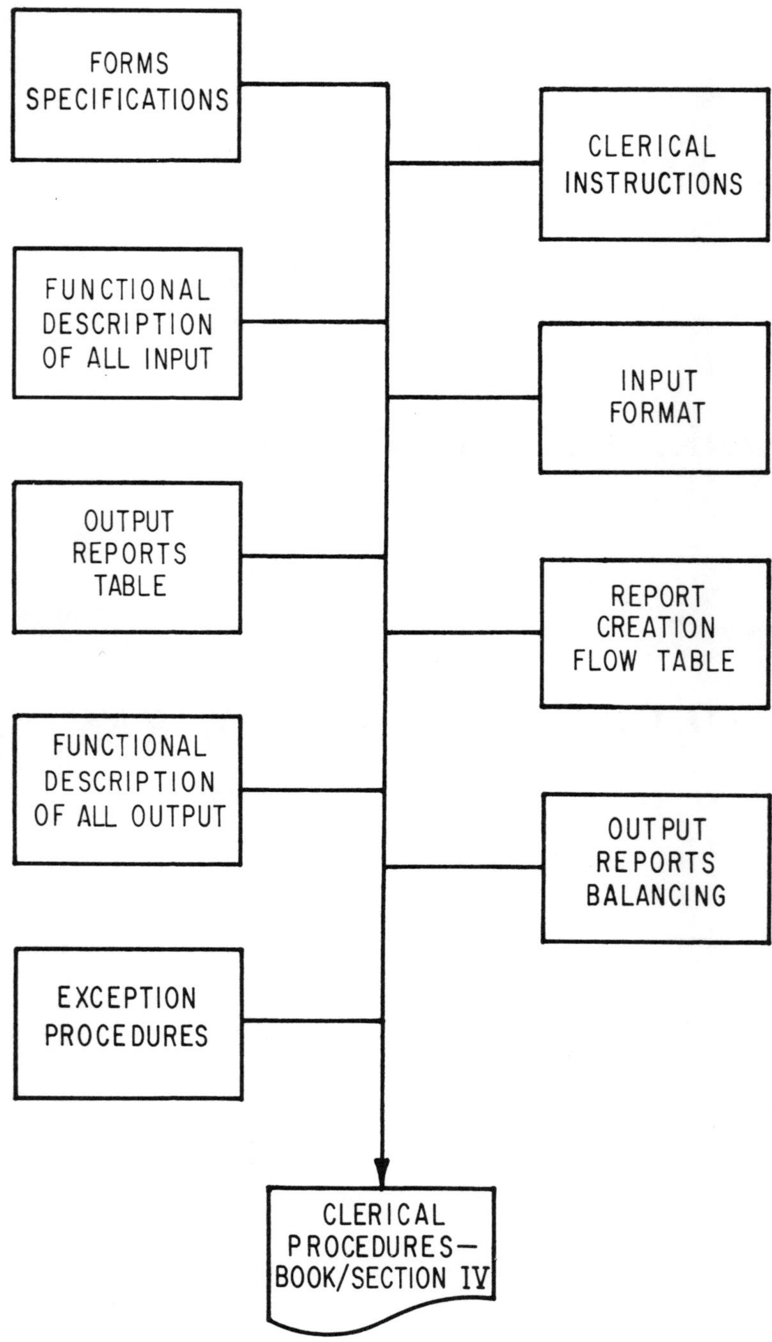

Figure 29. Organization of Book/Section IV: Clerical Procedures

CONTENTS

CLERICAL PROCEDURES (XX-000-CP/000-00)

This is a very important, albeit neglected, part of system documentation. It contains all information necessary to insure quality control in the various manual functions throughout the entire system cycle. Whether it is in a large or a small installation, the work of the clerk *before and after* computer operations can spell success or failure or at least the delay of a computer programming project. Since it is such an important phase, the forms used and procedures employed by the computer clerical personnel should be standardized.

FORMS SPECIFICATIONS (XX-000-CP/010-00)

a. *Functional Description* gives a clear, concise picture of the forms used–both in the input and the output phase, for example, Distribution Instructions form–in the particular system. The purpose of these preprinted forms is to state clearly whose responsibility it is to fill out specific forms, who verifies them, and where they are sent for processing. For example, "The 3 forms used by the Personnel Department's Computer Clerk to submit data to the PDB [Personnel Data Base System] are: MASTER FILE INPUT FORM, No. 069, used for changing a specific Master Employee File; JOB HISTORY & CLASSIFICATION FILES INPUT FORM, No. 070, used for changing either of these files; and REQUEST FOR SPECIAL PRINTOUTS FORM, No. 080, used for requesting various printouts." Another example: "After filling out the attached forms (when needed), the Computer Clerk writes his or her initials on the forms and gives them to the Verifying Clerk. The latter checks the forms' accuracy, including the transaction codes, the Requestor's signature, and an Authorization signature. After verifying the forms, she affixes her initials to them and sends them to the Computation Keypunch Section for processing."

Note: It is a good policy to have the personnel doing the clerical functions sign their initials on the work they do. The same principle applies here as on the previous documented sections. That is, by stating the name of the employee responsible for a certain phase of the particular computer system–whether it is the system analyst, the programmer, the data processing clerk, the keyboard or computer operator–a giant step is taken toward *Quality Assurance.* It is an accepted psychological fact that people will take more care with any work for which they are responsible if it bears their initials.

b. *Estimated Volume* is the quantity of the forms used by the particular computer system.
c. *Format* gives a detailed description of what is in each form, what transaction codes (T/C) are necessary, and what they mean. See Figures 31 and 32 for sample forms of Clerical Instructions and Distribution Instructions.
d. *Revision History* describes any revisions to the original forms; the date of each revision and a copy of the revised forms should be attached.
e. *Form Number and Name* is a list of each form and its assigned number exactly as it appears on the form.

CLERICAL INSTRUCTIONS (XX-000-CP/020-00)

a. *Keyboard Instructions* gives all the information keyboard operators need to know to keypunch from the completed forms whether on keypunch equipment, key-to-tape, or key-to-disk machines.
b. *Special Keyboard Instructions* tells the keyboard and verifying operators specific information they need to know about the particular system/program(s). For example, "The Master File update cards will be keypunched and verified on the swing shift and submitted to Sales Order Control System's SORT/EDIT program on a daily basis." Instruction is also given as to what type of codes are to be keypunched in what column. For example, "The first column must be the type code (A, E, or I, depending on which box is checked on the Grade/Salary Form, No. 25); columns 2-10 are the social security numbers (dashes omitted); column 11 a comma," and so forth.
c. *Retention Period* states how long certain files are to be retained—for example, "The Master File is to be retained for 5 days."; "Detail cards are retained by operations for 2 weeks."
d. *Processing Schedule* gives precise instructions when certain files are to be updated, when reports or other printed documents are to be distributed and to which departments, when transactions are to be coded, etc. For example: "All input transactions are to be coded and turned in to the keyboard operators at the end of the day shift."

FUNCTIONAL DESCRIPTION OF ALL INPUT (XX-000-CP/030-00)

This is a step-by-step description of each input item from the time it arrives at the clerk's desk until the clerk signs his initials on the document and gives it to the person at the next stage in the system cycle. In addition, a procedure chart (see Figure 30) is recommended for visual aid.

a. *Background Information* is narrative description of the source of input (input name and source), source documents (form names and numbers), input methods, files, and their functions.

b. *Minimum Input* states elements that all inputs in a particular system must contain, as well as the different types of records various programs accept as input. For example (1) transaction code, and (2) control information such as device number, sales order number, and item number.

c. *Additions* covers either the procedure for adding a new record to the file or the procedure for adding to a record already existing in the file. For example, "If it is an addition to the Sales Order, give the next item number in sequence."

d. *Changes* explains the procedure for making changes within a record.

e. *Deletions* describes the procedure for deleting a record or part of a record from the file. For example, "To delete a record from the Sales Order file use T/C 108 and fill out the Date, Quantity, Device No., Item, Job Order No., Description, and Customer."

f. *Cut-Off Date* specifies the exact date and time after which the clerk cannot accept input into the particular computer system. For example, "The San Francisco Data Center's cut-off date for receiving the Burton Warehouse reports is each Monday night at 10 p.m. Anything received after that time is processed in the next week's run."

g. *Procedure for Emergencies* tells the data processing clerk exactly what to do and whom to call in case of an emergency.

h. *Data Discipline* instructs personnel how to insure the reliability and accuracy of input data. While the forms used must be designed with simplicity and logic in mind, data processing clerks must be trained to adopt habits that make for reliable and accurate input.

INPUT FORMAT (XX-000-CP/040-00)

This section describes the input media format for each operation to be performed with the files. It also discusses how the system responds to the various formats. It differs from the Keyboard

Instructions by discussing the input media formats independently of the input forms (source documents).

This section can also contain detailed file tables. These tables list all the fields within the file records and give the following information for each field: field name, transaction code, type of data, number of positions (characters), and number of bytes. Each table can be preceded by an explanatory introduction to the file and the tables.

OUTPUT REPORTS TABLE (XX-000-CP/050-00)

The Output Reports table provides the following information for each report produced by the system: position (line position on the printout page), field name (for each field printed), and description (of the data in the field).

OUTPUT CREATION FLOW TABLE (XX-000-CP/060-00)

This is a table showing the names of the output media, such as reports, other printed documents, graphic and CRT displays, files, disk, etc., the programs that produce the output, the input files, and the disposition of the output. (This is a duplicate of GS/050, Figure 7.)

FUNCTIONAL DESCRIPTION OF ALL THE OUTPUT (XX-000-CP/070-00)

This is a detailed description of the output procedures as handled by the clerk.

a. *Name of Report/Statement, etc.,* gives the names of the output.
b. *Purpose* indicates the data the output contains, for example, "Invalid Data and Exception Report contains items that did not process, and gives the codes that explain why the items did not process."
c. *Type* gives the general nature of the data in the output, for example, statistical, informative, etc.
d. *Source* states the name of the program that generates the output.
e. *Distribution* indicates the destination of the output, that is, the department and/or offices the reports or other printed documents have to be sent to.
f. *Frequency* states how often the report is produced, for example, "The Device/Sales Status Report is generated daily."
g. *Volume* gives the number of copies of the output.

h. *Format* describes the layout of the report and gives instructions whether the report is to be decollated, burst, or bound. (See Figure 32.)

OUTPUT REPORTS BALANCING (XX-000-CP/080-00)

This is a matrix chart that cross-references information for all the reports produced by the system: name, description, frequency, number of copies, disposition, and reconciling action.

EXCEPTION PROCEDURES (XX-000-CP/090-00)

This section describes step by step the procedures to be followed in case of exceptional occurrences in the system activity, which relate to clerical procedures.

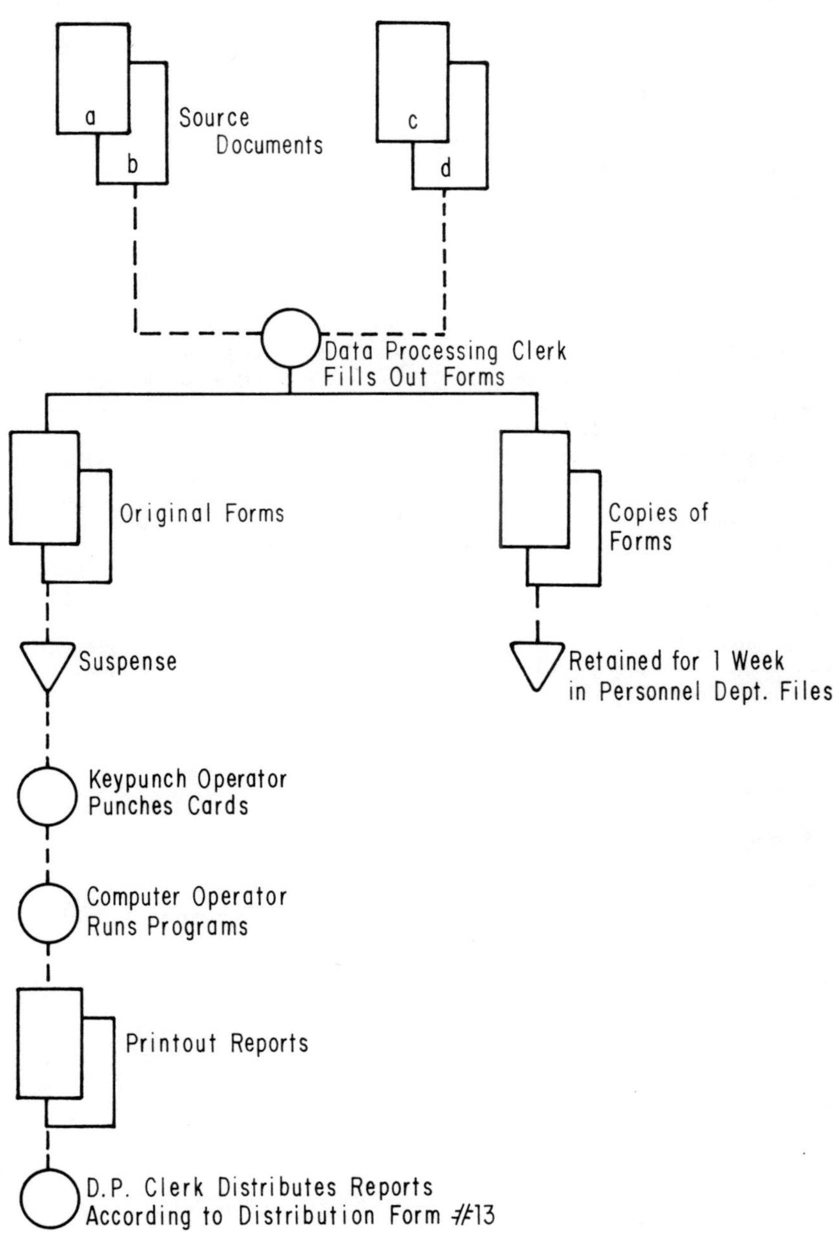

Figure 30. Procedure Chart

XX-000-CP/110-00
Date
Company/Division

JOB NAME:	**Job No.**	**Est. Vol.**	**Est. Time**
OPT	532	0-50	

Function*	**Symbol**	**Type****	**Card Form:**
Duplicate Punch Skip Verify	D P S V	A = alphabetic N = numeric A/N = alphanumeric	Number ______ Name Stock Color Yellow

SOURCE DOCUMENT USED: Promotional/Seasonal Changes	DISPOSITION OF CARDS: U.P. Can
RECEIVED FROM: Production Planning-Converting	DISPOSITION OF DOCUMENTS: Production Planning-Converting

CARD FIELD	**COLUMNS**		**FUNCTION***	**TYPE****	**REMARKS**
	From	**To**			
1. Warehouse	1	2	D	A	Always present
2. Blank	3	6			
3. Transaction Code	7	8	P & V	N	Constant "21"–Seasonal "22"–Promotional
4. Product Code	9	14	P & V	N	Always present
5. Weekly Code	15	16	P & V	N	Always present
6. Index	17	22	P & V	A/N	Always present
7. Blank	23	63			
8. Constant	64	64	D	N	"Ø" (zero)
9.					
10.					
11.					
12.					

Date: __________ Keypunch Clerk Name: S.A.

Figure 31. Keypunching and Verifying Instructions. Through the courtesy of Crown Zellerbach Corporation.

XX-000-CP/010-00
Date
Company/Division

SYSTEM NAME: BATHEL Inventory Control System REPORT NAME: Order Report						
REPORT NO. 531-101			FREQUENCY: Weekly			
DISTRIBUTION CLERK NAME: Joan Kelly						
1st COPY:	DECOLLATE	X	BURST		BIND	
DESTINATION: Via Freight–Production Planning OP Converting						
2nd COPY:	DECOLLATE	X	BURST		BIND	
DESTINATION: Production Planning–Bill Nash, Room 297						
3rd COPY:	DECOLLATE		BURST		BIND	
ADDITIONAL INSTRUCTIONS:						

Figure 32. Distribution Instructions. Through the courtesy of Crown Zellerbach Corporation

PDB-107-CP/000–00*
Date
Company/Division

SAMPLE APPLICATION:

PERSONNEL DATA BASE SYSTEM—CLERICAL PROCEDURES

*For the index key, please see the Introduction.

PDB-107-CP/000-00
Date
Company/Division

SAMP

CONTENTS

PDB-107-CP/000-00*
Date
Company/Division

SAMPLE

System No. & Name: PDP-101, PERSONNEL DATA BASE SYSTEM Date:

Data Processing Clerk: (Name) Keyboard Operator: (Name)

Items required and contained in this book/section	Yes	No	Comments (If no is checked)
1. Procedure Chart	✓		
2. Forms Specifications	✓		
3. Clerical Instructions	✓		
4. Keyboard Instructions	✓		
5. Description of Input	✓		
6. Input Format		✓	This is described in detail in the CP Book of the PIS (101)
7. Output Reports Table		✓	Reason identical with the above.
8. Exception Procedures	✓		

Figure 33. Documentation Checklist

*PDB is a subsystem under PERSONNEL INFORMATION SYSTEM, 101.

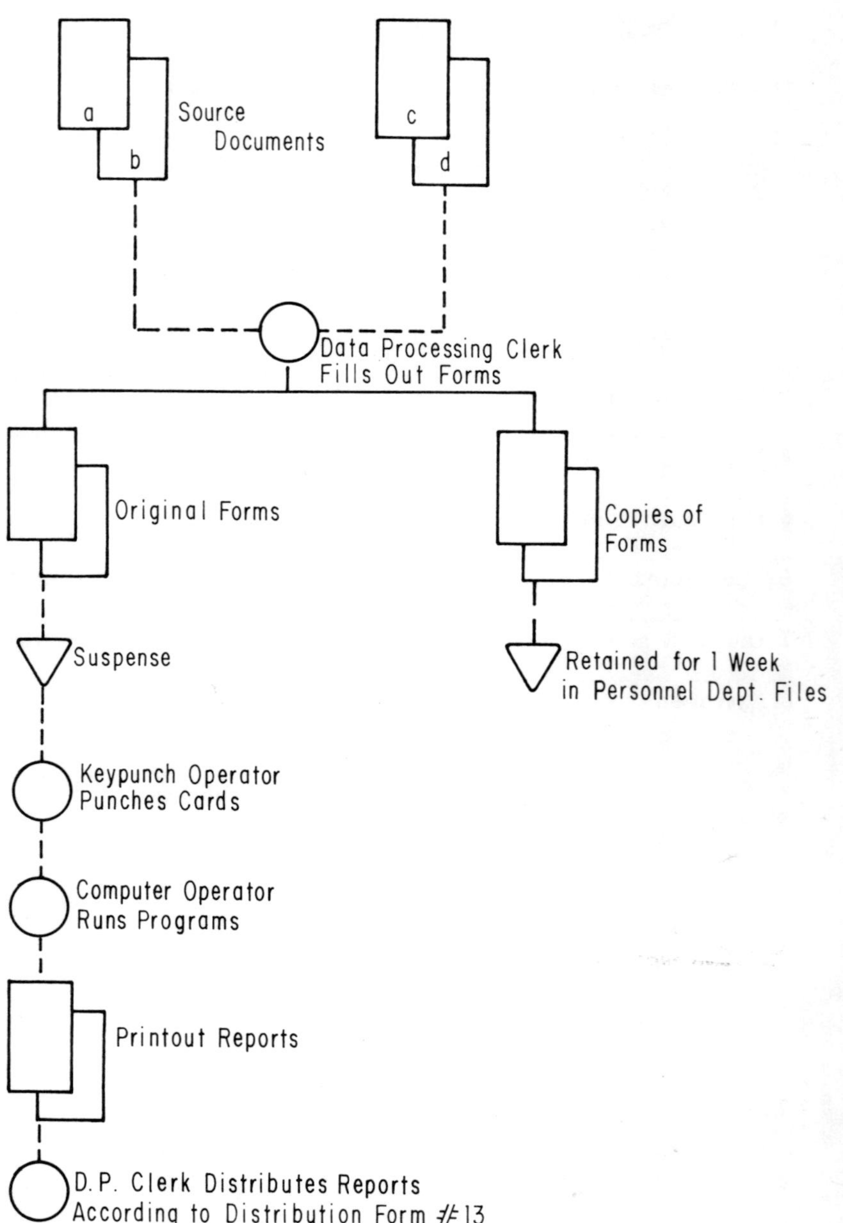

Figure 34. Procedure Chart

PDB-107-CP/010-00
Date
Company/Division

SAMPLE

FORMS SPECIFICATIONS (PDB-107-CP/010-00)

a. Functional Description

The Personnel Department of the Manufacturing Division uses three standardized forms for inputing data to the Personnel Data Base System: the Master File Input Form #10, the Progress File Input Form #11, and the Request for Special Printouts Form #12.

The Master File Input Form. Used to set up and specify how the Master Employee File is to be changed. (See sample form in Figure 35.)

The Progress File Input Form. Used for specifying how the Progress Employee File is to be changed. (See sample form in Figure 36.)

The Request for Special Printouts Form. Used when the need arises for special printouts of certain employee files. (See sample form in Figure 37.)

After filling out these forms (check that the requestor's signature, the department's number, and the date are included), the personnel department computer clerk puts his initials on the documents, puts them in a special container, and gives them to the keyboard operator.

After the cards have been punched and verified, they are sent to the computation center for processing. (Keyboard instructions are given below.)

In the output phase of this computer system, there is the Distribution Instructions Form #13. (For sample form see Figure 32.)

b. Estimated Volume

The estimated volume is 030 per form for the first three forms and 050 for the last form.

c. Format

The first two forms (10 and 11) have the following information across the page: a transaction code (T/C) and control information such as social security, employee name and number, and job grade. (Great care must be taken to enter the social security number correctly. A wrong digit will necessitate filling out the entire form again and resubmitting it.

PDB-107-CP/010-00
Date
Company/Division

The T/C *063 Setup* means a new employee; *064 Change* and *065 Delete* are self-explanatory.

The S.S. is social security and is written *without* a hyphen between the digits.

The rest of the column headings are self-explanatory.

On Form #12, check in the appropriate box for the file to be printed out according to the request.

PDB-107-CP/020-00
Date
Company/Division

SAMPLE

CLERICAL INSTRUCTIONS (PDB-107-CP/020-00)

a. Keyboard Instructions

Punch the appropriate T/C. If it is a 063 (Setup), punch all columns across the page. If it is a 064 (Change), punch only columns indicated. If 065 (Delete), punch the checked columns. If the form is *not* filled out correctly, place it in the REJECT box for the data processing clerk, who will redo all incorrect forms and resubmit them.

Do not submit any jobs to the computer operator until all deck cards have been punched and verified and your initials are affixed to the cover card that bears the job label.

b. Special Keyboard Instructions

The Master File and Progress File update cards are to be keypunched and verified each Monday night on the graveyard shift. The cards are to be labeled "Job PDP" and submitted to the computer operator for the Personnel Data Base System's CAPTURE/SORT/EDIT program on a weekly basis.

c. Retention Period

Detail cards are retained by the computation center operations for two weeks.

d. Processing Schedule

1. Input: all transactions are to be coded on Forms 10, 11, and 12 and submitted to the keyboard operators at the end of each Monday day shift.
2. The PDP Master File is to be updated weekly and the reports ready for distribution by 8:30 a.m. each Monday.

PDB-107-CP/030-00
Date
Company/Division

SAM

FUNCTIONAL DESCRIPTION OF ALL INPUT

a. Background Information

Input to the system is punched cards in free format. All inputs must have as a minimum: (1) a transaction code (T/C) and (2) control information that consists of a social security number, employee name and number, and job grade. The CAPTURE/ SORT/EDIT program accepts two different types of records:

1. Line Item (T/C: 060 = Setup, 061 = Change, 062 = Delete).
   This record is maintained by the Personnel Department of the Manufacturing Division and contains comprehensive information about the employee.
2. Progress (T/C: 063 = Setup, 064 = Change, 065 = Delete).
   This record is maintained by the Personnel Department of the Manufacturing Division and contains data about the progress of the employee.

PDB-107-CP/040-00
Date
Company/Division

SAMPLE

FUNCTIONAL DESCRIPTION OF ALL OUTPUT (PDB-101-CP/040-00)

There are five reports generated by this system, whose purpose it is to maintain status reports on all employees.

a. Employee History Report.

This report is generated weekly.

1. *Purpose.* Complete status employee information
2. *Type.* Informational
3. *Source.* POSTING Program
4. *Distribution.* Personnel department
5. *Frequency.* Weekly and as needed

b. Employee Progress Report.

1. *Purpose.* Status information on employee progress
2. *Type.* Informational
3. *Source.* POSTING Program
4. *Distribution.* Personnel department
5. *Frequency.* Weekly and as needed

c. Grade/Salary Report.

1. *Purpose.* Status information on employee job grade and salary
2. *Type.* Informational
3. *Source.* POSTING Program
4. *Distribution.* Personnel Department
5. *Frequency.* Weekly and as needed

d. Control Report.

1. *Purpose.* Presents statistics about what was done during the run and about the current contents of the Master Employee and Progress Files

2. *Type.* Statistical
3. *Source.* POSTING program
4. *Distribution.* Personnel, Payroll, and Auditor Departments
5. *Frequency.* Every run

e. Exception Report

1. *Purpose.* Listing of items that did not process, plus codes indicating why items did not process
2. *Type.* Error and compare
3. *Source.* EDIT and POSTING programs
4. *Distribution.* Personnel department
5. *Frequency.* Every run

PDB-107-CP/050-00 SAMPLE
Date
Company/Division

EXCEPTION PROCEDURES (PDP-107-CP/050-00)

a. For the Data Processing Clerk

If source documents such as copies of employee applications or other documents from the Personnel Clerk are smirched or otherwise unclear or not consistent (social security number or other vital statistics differing from one page to another), the Data Processing Clerk should reject such source documents and return them to the Personnel Clerk whose initials are on the documents. Unclear source documents should be requested to be resubmitted. If no initials are found on the documents, they should be returned with a request for clear source documents to the personnel department supervisor.

b. For the Keypunch Operator

If any errors are found on any forms, the forms should be placed in the REJECT box; at the end of the keypunching of the deck, they should be returned to the Data Processing Clerk whose initials are on the appropriate line in the form. If there are no initials, the forms to be filled out again and resubmitted should be sent to the Data Processing Supervisor.

PDB-107-CP/010-00
Date
Company/Division

Item Record Transaction Codes
060 = Setup
061 = Change
062 = Delete

Data Processing Clerk ________

Form No. 10

Transaction Code	Social Security	Hire Date	Emp. Name	Address	Sex	Education	Marital Status	Home Phone	Emp. No.	Dept. No.	Job Grade	Comments
1 3	4 12	13 17	18 28	29 30	40	41 42	43	44 50	51 54	55 57	58 64	65
061		71271										Error in hire date

Legend: SEX, M = Male, F = Female; EDUCATION, HG = High School Graduate, BS/BA = Bachelor of Science or Bachelor of Arts Degree, MS/MA = Master of Science or Master of Arts degree; MARITAL STATUS, M = Married, S = Single, D = Divorced, W = Widowed.

Figure 35. Master File Input Item Record

SAMP

PDG-107-CP/010-00
Date
Company/Division

Data Record Transaction Codes
063 = Setup
064 = Change
065 = Delete

Data Processing Clerk ____________

Form No. 11

Transaction Code	Social Security	Emp. No.	Job Grade	Current Salary	Review Period #1	New Salary	Review Period #2	New Salary	Review Period #3	Comments
1 3	4 12	13 16	17 14	15 20	21 25	26 31	32 37	38 43	44 48	49
065		94301	2-58							Emp. terminated 4/12/71

Figure 36. Progress File Input Data Record

PDB-107-CP/010-00
Date
Company/Division

Data Processing Clerk________

Form No. 12

Generate a printout of the following file(s)

☐ MASTER FILE	Requested By:	Dept.	Date
	Approved By:	Dept.	Date
☐ PROGRESS FILE	Requested By:	Dept.	Date
	Approved By:	Dept.	Date
☐ GRADE/SALARY FILE	Requested By:	Dept.	Date
	Approved By:	Dept.	Date
THE FOLLOWING EMPLOYEE(S) RECORD(S)	Requested By:	Dept.	Date
	Approved By:	Dept.	Date

1. ______________________ 5. ______________________

2. ______________________ 6. ______________________

3. ______________________ 7. ______________________

4. ______________________ 8. ______________________

Checks in the appropriate boxes indicate which files are to have a nonscheduled, special printout(s).

Figure 37. Request for Nonscheduled, Special Printouts

SAM

BOOK/SECTION V

AUDIT CONTROL DESCRIPTION

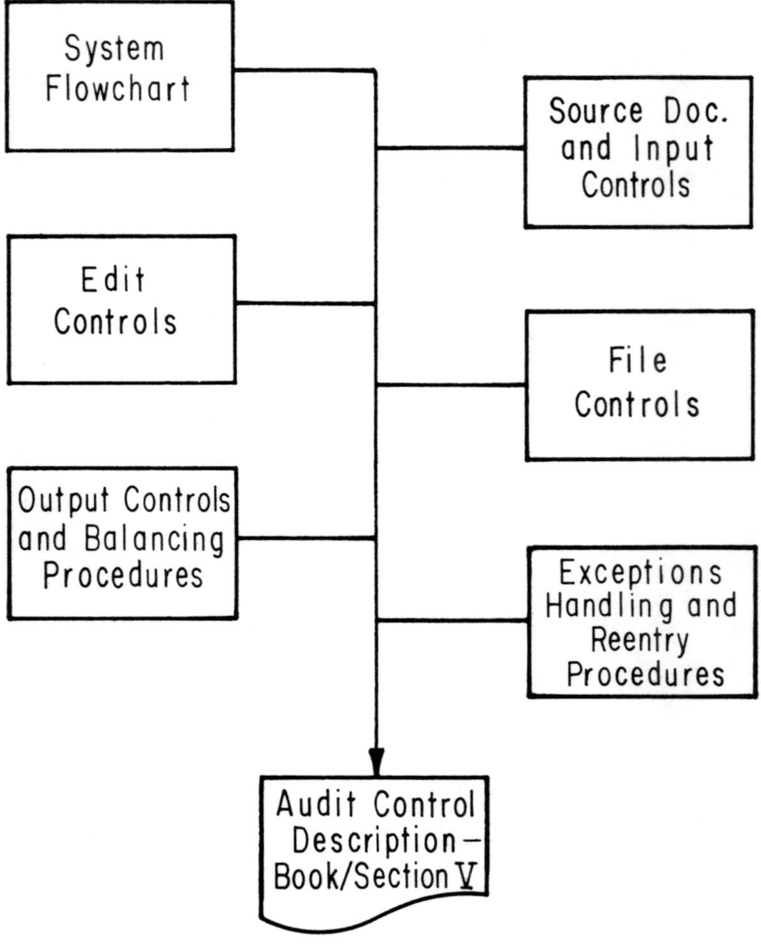

Figure 38. Organization of Book/Section V: Audit Control Description

CONTENTS

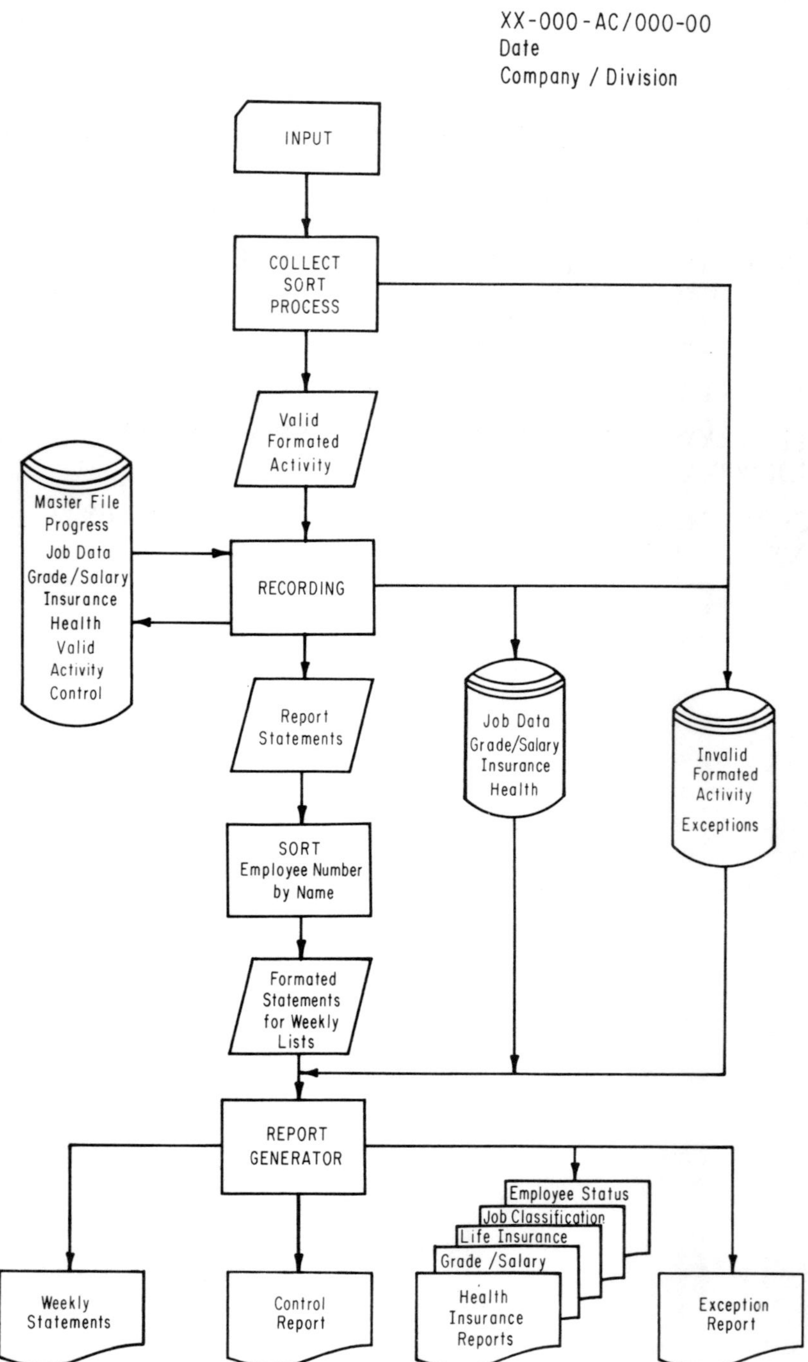

Figure 39. Sample System Flowchart

AUDIT CONTROL DESCRIPTION (XX-000-AC/000-00)

Internal and external auditors are perhaps more concerned with the control of business information than are computer professionals. Auditors have to know that data is processed efficiently and that the data they use in preparing various financial reports for management, stockholders, and government agencies are reliable. In other words, auditors are the *quality assurance* professionals of EDP Systems. They establish control criteria for the accounting data that is external to the computer as well as internal to it. The American Institute of Certified Public Accountants defines internal control as follows:

> Internal control comprises a plan of organization and all of the coordinate methods and measures adopted within a business to safeguard its assets, check the accuracy and reliability of its accounting data, promote operational efficiency, and encourage adherence to prescribed managerial policies.*

Correlatively, this section presents to auditors the information they need by lifting out and duplicating relevant data from documented portions of the previous phases of the system. Each application requires a somewhat different approach to programming controls; nevertheless, there are certain control criteria that may be used—with variations—with all systems.

Since the goals of systems designers and auditors are the same—effective, timely, reliable systems, whether for complex on-line, real time, batch-processing, or mini-computers—the two groups should work together. Moreover, it is the responsibility of the EDP documentation specialist or the EDP coordinator to compile the material for *Audit Control Description*. This book saves the auditors time they would normally spend searching through volumes of computer program listings and other documentation to trace the "audit trail," a difficult task at best in these days of highly sophisticated systems.

The information auditors need and which must be included in the Audit Control Description book consists of (a) procedures that verify the accuracy of data in the crucial, yet somewhat neglected, phase—input preparation; (b) identifying source documents and where certain data enter and exit the system; (c) which data are passed on to other systems; (d) the type of control records the system contains;

*Auditing Standards and Procedures, New York: American Institute of Certified Public Accountants, Inc., 1963, p. 27.

(e) how these data are checked for accuracy; and (f) the procedure for correcting errors.

Auditors should insist on proper external controls, for example, that preprinted input forms (used by EDP clerical personnel) be designed (or redesigned) as simply and functionally as possible, and that internal controls be incorporated into the system at the initial or system design phase, not wait when the system is operating (it might be too late then).

Incidentally, it is not too far fetched for auditors to ask to have the importance of meticulous care in handling EDP input emphasized during the employee orientation/training period.

Finally, it is extremely important to take proper measures to insure that whenever *any* part of a particular system is updated, the Auditor Control Description book be updated also.

SOURCE DOCUMENTS AND INPUT CONTROLS (XX-00-AC/010-00)

In order for the auditors to review the system, they need:

1. The system flow chart. This document can be duplicated from Book/Section I, General System, or Book/Section III, User's Manual, of the particular computer system.

2. Source documents used as input, for example, purchase requests form, priority rating form, sales order control input item record form, promotional/seasonal changes form, etc.

3. The function(s) of the particular source document(s) and the technique(s) used in verifying the correctness of the data after it is converted via punched cards, magnetic tape, key-to-disk, paper tape, or on-line terminal into acceptable input to the system. In short, auditors need to review the input controls such as the input data being read twice and, in case of any errors, the procedure to halt the processing. (This should be in addition to the manual control where the lead man/woman checks and verifies the work of several data processing clerks and keyboard personnel whose responsibility it is to prepare the input.) Relevant material, both for (2) and (3) can be found and duplicated from the documented Book/Section IV, Clerical Procedures, and Book/Section VI, Operator's Instructions.

4. The auditors need to know which program(s) or phase of the system handles the input, for example, "SORT/EDIT program captures the input for XYZ System," or "CAPTURE handles two types of input, original and reentry." The documented Book/Section III, Programming Specifications, contains this information for the auditors.

EDIT CONTROLS (XX-000-AC/020-00)

Here the auditors look for the proof that data (after the input data have been sorted and edited) are checked for validity. One way of handling this is to have the system designer or programmer write into the system a printout of Detail and Error List. This printout (intermediate results) can print not only the exceptions that occur during the SORT/EDIT processing, but also analyze the errors.

Details of this information are contained in Book/Section III, Programming Specifications. They are to be duplicated and included in this book/section.

FILE CONTROLS (XX-000-AC/030-00)

File controls are designed into the production program. Information on this phase of the system is found in Book/Section II, File and Input/Output Specifications. Relevant parts are to be duplicated and added to the Audit Control Description book.

Many systems have built-in control files generated by certain programs to be used as audit checkpoints. These files are then audited at the end of the day's processing to verify accuracy. For example, a Proof-of-Deposit computer system can be designed so that besides the company (total) control files there are control files for individual stores (if it is a chain store or manufacturer), or branches (if it is a bank or real estate corporation). There may be three types of control records for both company and store/branch: (1) for regular activity, (2) for additional activity, and (3) for deletion activity. These controls are then compared between EDIT and SORT programs and between SORT and MERGE programs, and they must all agree. If they are "out of proof," they are printed out on the exception reports. This is an effective file control technique of "proof totals" or "hash totals."

OUTPUT CONTROLS AND BALANCING PROCEDURES (XX-000-AC/040-00)

The control of output and balancing procedures can be achieved by well-designed control reports that give not only statistical data about the daily runs but also data about the size of the relevant files. Moreover, there should be a breakdown on the items *before and after* updating the master file. All the figures must agree, otherwise the data appears on the exception report. There can also be a "cross-index" output balancing procedure. This is a matrix chart with data listed horizontally and vertically, where the result of the former must equal the result of the latter.

This data can be found and is to be duplicated from Book/ Section II, File and I/O Specifications, and Book/Section III, Programming Specifications.

EXCEPTIONS HANDLING AND REENTRY PROCEDURES (XX-000-AC/050-00)

It is essential for an efficient system that exception and reentry procedures be handled in a standard manner. There must be exception reports designed within the system. The reports list each run's invalid transactions. They show which items did not process; the error messages are printed out.

If it is a simple faulty input, the operator can repunch the card(s) (if the error does not extend to too many cards and of course if the input is via punched cards) and reenter the data. If the input is entered through OCR (optical card reader) and the error came about because the document was wrinkled or torn, making it impossible for the OCR to read it correctly, the computer operator has to take the data off the document and enter it via punched cards, key-to-tape or key-to-disk, and so forth. If, however, the system is down because of a program or machine malfunction, the system designer should anticipate such incidents and there should be a stand-alone program such as a disaster buffer print, which then prints the contents of the input and output buffers. The printout assists the reconcilers in locating the items sorted to a pocket but not recorded on disk because of failure. When the system resumes functioning, the data can be reentered through INPUT or REENTRY programs.

There is another method for the auditor, by which—if he is sufficiently knowledgeable about the computer programming—can review the system. This involves having the keyboard operator punch and verify two sets of cards (if the input to the system is via punched cards), the data processing clerk prepare two sets of tapes (if the input to the system is via key-to-tape device), and so on. One set of input data goes into the company's production program, while the other set of input data is channeled into the auditor's program. If the output of the auditor's program agrees with the company's program—besides a certain number of approved exceptions—the auditor accepts the program as reliable. Otherwise the program has to be debugged or even revised.

There are many drawbacks to this method. One of the most obvious is that an auditor does not have the time or the inclination to spend all of his working hours programming. Also, whether the organization is a large or a small computer installation, it is not economical for it to prepare two sets of input and to run two sets of programs, even on a selective basis. Consideration of all of these factors is a good reason for advocating the previous audit control techniques and only mentioning the above method.

BOOK/SECTION VI

OPERATOR'S INSTRUCTIONS

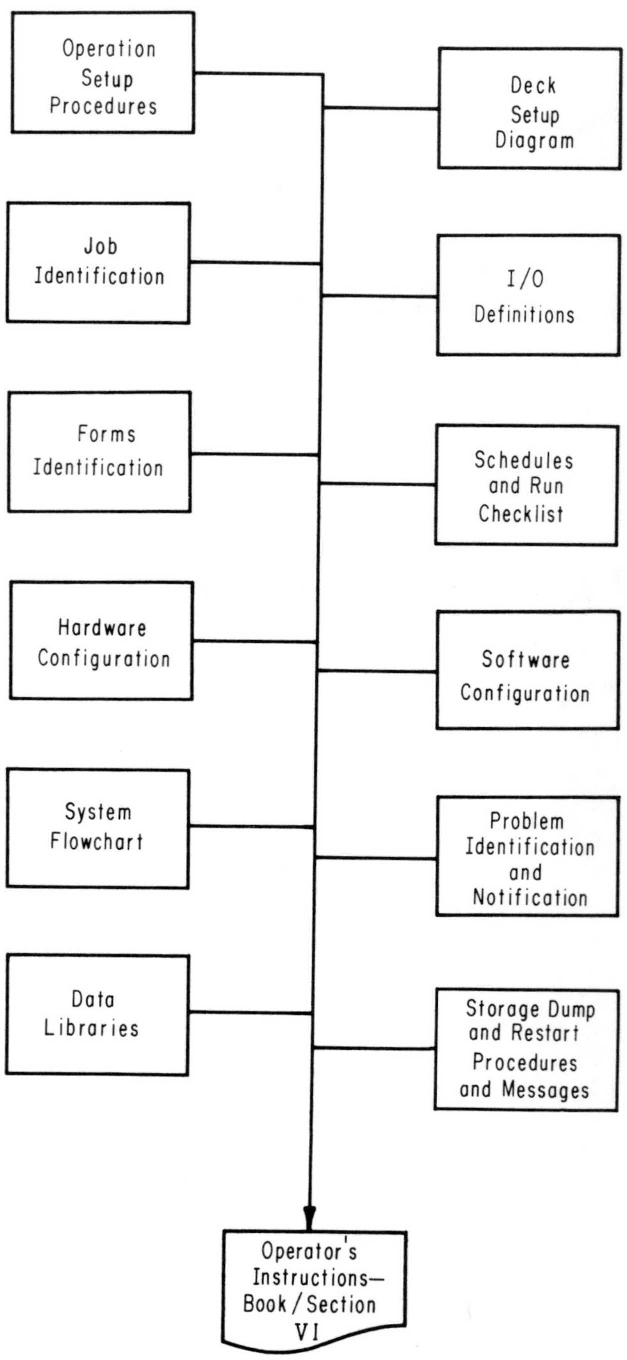

Figure 40. Organization of Book/Section VI: Operator's Instructions

CONTENTS

OPERATOR'S INSTRUCTIONS (XX-000-OI/000-00)

The instructions to the computer operator should be one of the most comprehensive and detailed book/section in the documentation manual of any system. The Operator's Instructions (or Run Book) consist of an abstract that describes the purpose and use of the particular computer system and a procedure description providing precise instructions.

The reason for emphasizing the necessity to give detailed instructions to the operator is that the operation phase of the computer system can make or break the particular system if not the computer facility. For the same reason, the data operations supervisor should *not* accept any job (no matter what crisis-story the programmer comes with) unless the job is accompanied by a documentation acceptance checklist form–all filled out. (For a sample form see Figure 46.)

OPERATION SETUP PROCEDURES (XX-000-OI/010-00)

To insure that correct setup procedures or standards are followed, the instructions must be explicit. For example: "Pick up cards from Keypunch. Check the Job Card. This card is blue with no corners cut. A set-up card follows. If the Job and the Setup cards are not the first and second cards in the deck, return the deck *unprocessed* to the programmer/user." A deck setup diagram, such as in Figure 41, is recommended as well as peripheral equipment setup forms (see Clerical Procedures, Forms Specifications).

It is the responsibility of the computer operator to check the Console Log daily *prior to operation set-up* and when taking over the shift. Cancel and return improperly set up jobs to the user; give reason(s) in the Communication Log for cancelling jobs and enter messages in the console log for reference before shift turnover. That is, give an explanation whenever, because of a hardware failure or software error, the system is down or a job is cancelled by the system because it exceeds the given time.

JOB IDENTIFICATION (XX-000-OI/020-00)

A good way to identify incoming work and at the same time

establish the date and time the computer operations received the job is to have a small time-clock type of machine. This machine prints sequence numbers and time and date label, which the operator can then paste on the outside of the box containing the data deck. If computer operations does not have this machine, the operator can mark manually the sequence number and time and date on the outside of the deck card box.

INPUT/OUTPUT DEFINITIONS (XX-000-OI/030-00)

This subsection is a duplication of the I/O Definitions, Layouts of All Files, and I/O Records (PS/040) of Book/Section III, Programming Specifications. Consequently, for all information about input format, file identification, etc., Book/Section III, PS/040, should be consulted. If that is not feasible, it should be duplicated and inserted here.

FORMS IDENTIFICATION (XX-000-OI/040-00)

The computer operator needs to know whether the output of a particular system is going to be printed on standard 1-ply ruled paper, 2-ply blank stock, or nonstandard. For example, "Put 5-part ruled stock in printer when SPO asks for it."

Also, the output peripherals have to be specified, for example, printers are designated as SYSOUT or SYSPRT; punches are designated as SYSPCH.

SCHEDULES (XX-000-OI/050-00)

For each job, a schedule has to be established so that the computer operator can follow a specific pattern and thus insure proper turnaround time and procedure consistency. This subsection includes:

a. *Run Frequency* of each job, for example, "The Sales Order Control System is operated daily to maintain an up-to-date sales order file and produce daily reports."
b. *Processing Deadline* states the latest time the specific job can be started as well as the latest finish time. Also, whether it has priority over other jobs, for example, "The Master File is updated daily during the grave-yard shift, and reports are ready for distribution by 8:00 a.m."

c. *Run Time* states the maximum run time, for example, "Maximum run time is 10 minutes." Thus if the program runs over the specified time, the operator can cancel the job.
d. *Control Check Before Run–After Run.* For this control the computer operator must have a Production Run Checklist supplied by the programmer/user. A Run checklist provides the tool for controlling the production runs before and after.
e. *Retention Periods* give specific instructions about what to do with the tapes or disk that are created during the run and how long their retention cycles are. For example, "Label output tape 'SOCTIL' and use it to store Library Maintenance Dump. A tape is reserved for each day of the week."
f. *Priority* states the high or low priority number assigned to the task.
g. *Run Checklist Form.* This form (see Figure 42), incorporates all of the above essential features.

HARDWARE CONFIGURATION (XX-000-01/060-00)

The computer operator needs to know the hardware configuration for the particular system, especially if there is more than one CPU on the premise. This also includes the peripheral devices the system uses. For example, "XYZ System runs on IBM 360/22 (a stripped down 360/30), core size 32K maximum, Card/Reader Puncher #2540, Disk Storage #2311, 2401 Tape Driver, Printer #1403, and it operates under DOS."

SOFTWARE CONFIGURATION (XX-000-01/070-00)

This subsection states not only what language the programs are written in, what programs and files the particular system consists of, but also the operating system (OS, MCP, DOS), and the flow of the system, so that the computer operator knows the sequence of processing plus the features of the system. For example, "SOC System consists of 3 COBOL programs: SORT/EDIT (input), UPDATE, and REPORT GENERATOR. The sequence of execution and file handling is controlled by the programmed flow of operations."

A duplicate of the system flowchart, taken from Book I, General System, is included here.

REFERENCE CHART OF PROGRAMS AND FILES (XX-000-OI/080-00)

Since this reference chart—showing which programs use which files—is already included in Book I, General System (see PER-101-GS/030-00), it is a good idea to duplicate this matrix chart and insert it in this book for additional information about the operating system for the computer operator.

OUTPUT CREATION FLOW TABLE (XX-000-OI/090-00)

The same principle applies to this subsection. The computer operator needs this information. Moreover, this chart can also be duplicated from Book/Section I (see PER-101-GS/040-00) and insert it here.

PROBLEM IDENTIFICATION AND NOTIFICATION (XX-000-OI/100-00)

For maintaining operating consistency and data discipline during swing and graveyard shifts, weekends and holidays and personnel turnover periods, it is essential that the Operator's Instructions book contain precise information on the above. That is, the operator must document the problem (with his name and the time the problem occurred) on the tape recorder and/or card besides the log book. Second, there should be a list of people he can contact at various times. Of course, if there are any personnel changes, it should be noted here immediately. Keeping this section of the operator's book updated is crucial. Also, the operator must know that if it is a hardware problem he encounters, who the hardware manufacturer's maintenance engineer is whom he can contact at any hour. All computer manufacturers assign maintenance engineers to customer computer facilities. These engineers are always "on call" in case of hardware failures.

DATA LIBRARIES (XX-000-OI/110-00)

The computer operator needs to know the types of user libraries that are maintained by the facility—test procedures, SYS PROCLIB, etc.—and what methods are allowed for the user to update the libraries. Thus the operator can control the updating procedures.

Also, specific instructions must be given in regard to storing library cards, paper tapes, magnetic tapes, and disks, for example,

"XYZ tapes are reserved and stored with the permanent library tapes. These tapes are used only as XYZ Library Dumps. The tapes are stored by date: latest date–first tape on the left; oldest date, last tape on the right. They are rotated daily. The oldest date, then, becomes the latest dump tape."

STORAGE DUMP AND RESTART PROCEDURES (XX-000-OI/120-00)

If the system goes down, for whatever reason, a storage dump is necessary before the system can be restarted. Consequently, a step-by-step instruction must be given to the computer operator about how to use the storage dump program (most facilities have one), then how to restart the operations. For example, "Depress the STOP and LOAD switches on the PDP-9. This will dump core onto the Dump Tape on the NOVA. Then load SOC-UP and SOC-WE from the latest SOCTIL tape. (Your log book will indicate the latest tape.) Finally, reexecute SOC-IN."

MISCELLANEOUS OPERATING INSTRUCTIONS (XX-000-OI/130-00)

This is a catch-all for any additional information that is not covered in any of the previous subsections–for example, ERROR MESSAGES.

System Name & Number:

Program Name & Number: Programmer Name:

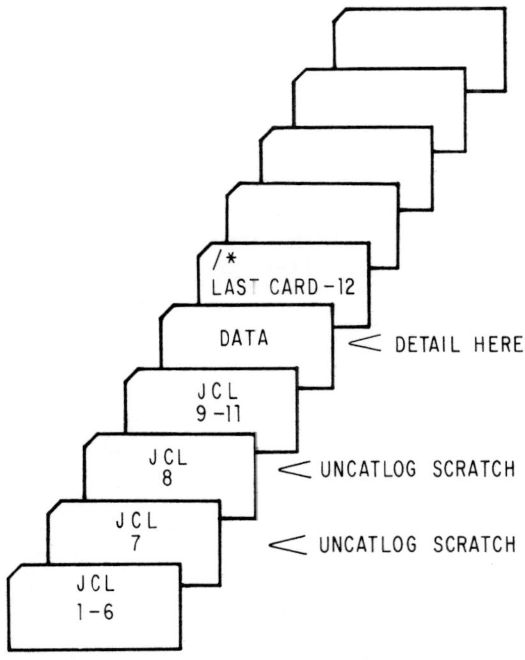

(This deck setup sample is for a program run on the IBM 360/50)

Figure 41. Deck Setup Diagram (XX-000-OI/010-00). Through the courtesy of Crown Zellerbach Corporation.

XX-000-OI/050-00
Date
Company/Division

System Name & No ____________ Job Name & No. ____________ Step No. ____________

INPUT RUN FREQUENCY RETENTION

PROCESSING DEADLINE ______________ PRIORITY NO. ____________________

ESTIMATED RUN TIME ______________ CONTROLS ____________________

OUTPUT RUN FREQUENCY RETENTION

PROCESSING DEADLINE ______________ PRIORITY NO. ____________________

ESTIMATED RUN TIME ______________ CONTROLS ____________________

RESTART PROCEDURE

Computer Operator (Name): ____________________

Figure 42. Run Checklist Form

BAT-105-0I/000-00*
Date
Company/Division

SAMPLE APPLICATION:

BATHEL INVENTORY CONTROL SYSTEM—OPERATOR'S INSTRUCTIONS

*For the index key, please see the Introduction.

SAM

CONTENTS

BAT-105-0I/000-00
Date
Company/Division

SAMPLE

System No. & Name: BAT-105, BATHEL Inventory Control System Date:

System Analyst(s) Programmer/User Name & Ext. No.:

Items required and contained in this book/section	Yes	No	Comments (if no is checked)
1. System Flowchart and General System Concepts and Purpose	✓		
2. Operation Setup Procedures	✓		
3. Deck Setup Diagram	✓		
4. Clerical Procedures		✓	See Book/Section IV—Clercial Procedures
5. I/O Definitions		✓	See Book/Section III—Programming Specifications
6. Schedules	✓		
7. Checklist for Run	✓		
8. Hardware Configuration	✓		
9. Software Configuration	✓		
10. System Error Messages	✓		
11. Library Setup	✓		
12. Input Formats	✓		
13. Parameters for Macro Routine		✓	No Required for this System
14. Available Options	✓		
15. Core Dump and Restart Procedures	✓		

Figure 43. Documentation Acceptance Checklist

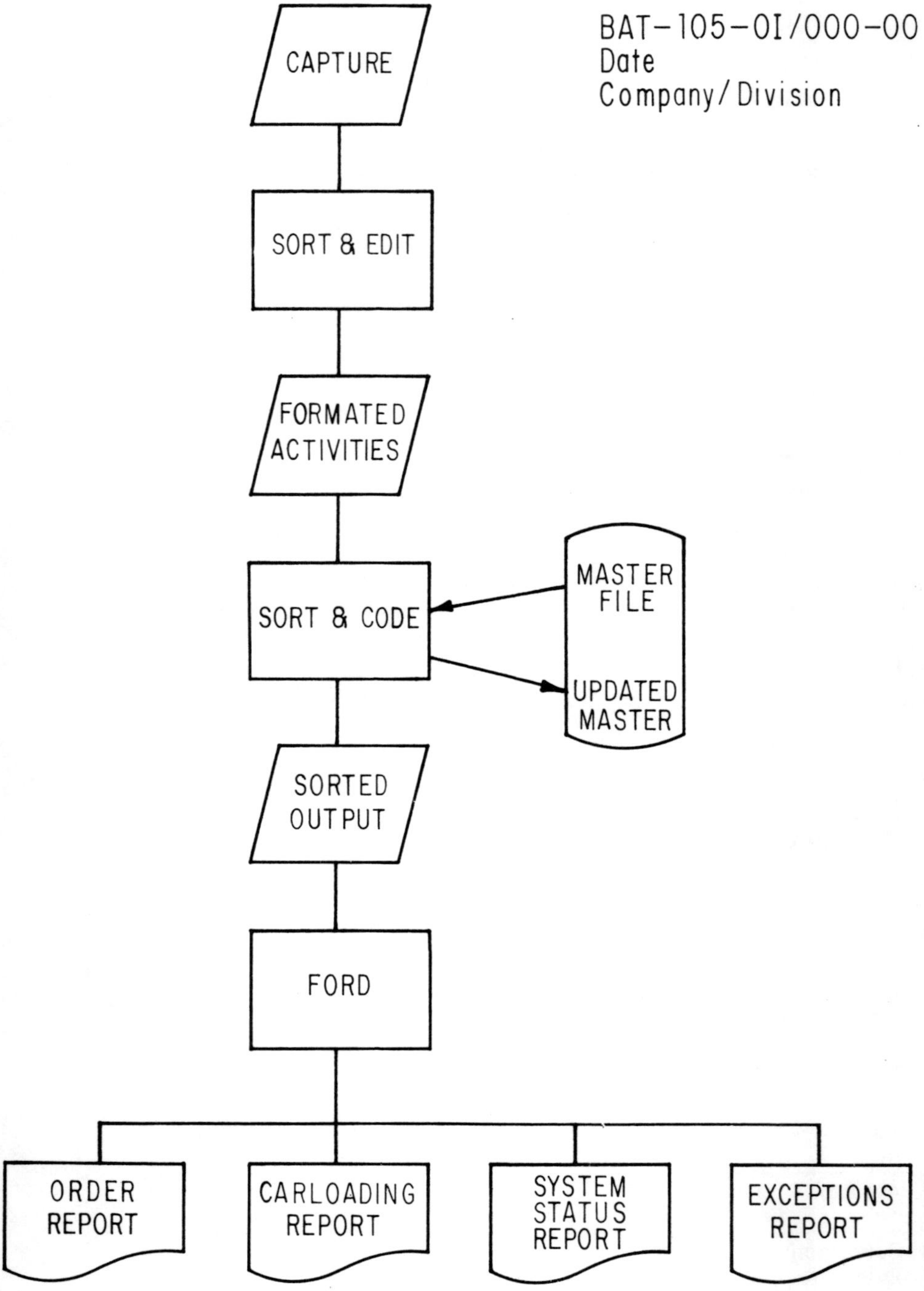

BAT-105-0I/000-00
Date
Company/Division

CAPTURE

SORT & EDIT

FORMATED ACTIVITIES

SORT & CODE

MASTER FILE

UPDATED MASTER

SORTED OUTPUT

FORD

ORDER REPORT

CARLOADING REPORT

SYSTEM STATUS REPORT

EXCEPTIONS REPORT

Figure 44. System Flowchart. Through the courtesy of Crown Zellerbach Corporation.

BAT-105-0I/000-00
Date
Company/Division

SAMPLE

OPERATOR'S INSTRUCTIONS (BAT-105-0I/000-00)

Abstract

The BATHEL Inventory Control System, a subsystem of Management Information Systems, is designed to provide a weekly guidance for the Consumer Products Sales Division in ordering items and certain distributor sales items needed to serve the BATHEL sales area. The system generates recommended order quantities and carloading patterns based on weekly shipments from the BATHEL warehouse.

The system consists of three programs: SORT & EDIT, SORT & CODE, and FORD (a weekly report generator). The system flow is in the following sequence: CAPTURE takes input data that indicates the warehouse activity during the week and its current inventory status, as well as the control information. SORT & EDIT processes the data. FORMATED ACTIVITIES add a master file record for a product item, change an existing product item in the file, alter the promotional or seasonal indices, delete the file for any product item. SORTED OUTPUT takes the new updated data and passes it on to FORD, which then generates weekly the order, carloading, and exception reports, and monthly (and on request), the system status report. (See Figure 44, System Flowchart.)

BAT-105-0I/010-00
Date
Company/Division

OPERATION SETUP PROCEDURES (BAT-105-0I/000-00)

a. *Get cards from Keypunch.* Cards will be labelled "Job 532."

b. *Check for invalid card input.* Also check for keypunch errors.

c. *If there are no errors*, insert detail cards behind JCL 1–6, as per the deck setup diagram for a normal run, in Figure 46.

d. *If errors are significant*, correct errors (punch new cards) and rerun. See Figures 48 and 49. If errors are not significant, use as is and rerun at a later date. (Reruns though must be made before next weekly run.)

e. *Execute CAPTURE.*

f. *Put Standard Wide 2-part paper in printer* when report generator is ready.

g. *Label output tape* "FORD, Job 532" and store it in Table Library.

h. *Store details cards by date.*

i. *Distribute reports per distribution procedure.* See Figure 49.

j. *All additional information* can be found on the 360 computer setup form, Figure 45.

BAT-105-0I/020-00
Date
Company/Division

SAMPLE

Job No. 532	Step No. 5001	Report No. 101	Job Name: FORD NORMAL RUN	Run Time: 8 minutes Frequency: Weekly*

1403 Printer

Forms:		Form Alignment:	
Name:	Standard Wide Stock	First Print Position	Normal
No.	1413	Last Print Position	Normal
Parts	2	First Print Line	Normal

Carriage Tape: Job: Standard Short Step: ________

Printer Setting: Density: Normal Thickness: Normal

2540 Reader Punch

Punch:		Reader:	
Card name	None	Program No.	532-5001
Card no.		Card Used	
Card color			
		Recd from	Data Assembly

P1	P2	RP	R2	R1
Name	Name	Name	Name	Name
Disposition	Disposition	Disposition	Disposition	Disposition Data Assembly
none	none	none	none	

23XX Disk Drives Pack No.: ØPRS01	24XX Tape Drives (files in order called for) File Name and No.: Input Tapes — File Name and No.: Output Tapes
	Computer Operator (Name):

*On Monday nights.

Figure 45. 360 Computer Setup—A. Through the courtesy of Crown Zellerbach Corporation.

BAT-105-0I/030-00
Date
Company/Division

SAMP

JOB NO. 532 STEP 5001

JOB NAME: FORD (Normal Run) COMPUTER OPERATOR NAME:

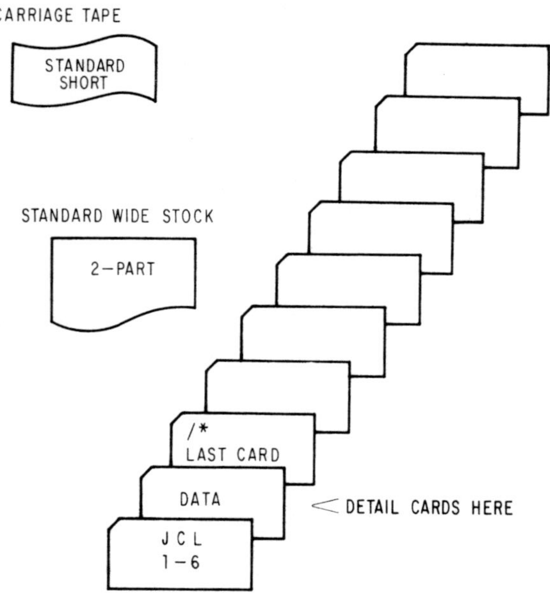

Figure 46. Deck Setup Diagram—A. Through the courtesy of Crown Zellerbach Corporation.

BAT-105-0I/040-00
Date
Company/Division

SAMPLE

Job. No. 532	Step No. 5002	Report No. 101	Job Name: FORD RERUN	Run Time: 8 minutes Frequency: When Required*

1403 Printer

Forms:		Form Alignment:	
Name	Standard Wide Stock	First Print Position	Normal
No.	1413	Last Print Position	Normal
Parts	2	First Print Line	Normal

Carriage Tape: Job: Standard Short Step: ______

Printer Setting: Density: Normal Thickness: Normal

2540 Reader Punch

Punch:		Reader:	
Card name	None	Program No.	532-5002
Card No.		Card used	
Card color			
		Recd from	Data Assembly

P1	P2	RP	R2	R1
Name	Name	Name	Name	Name
Disposition	Disposition	Disposition	Disposition	Disposition Data Assembly
none	none	none	none	

23XX Disk Drives Pack No.:	24XX Tape Drives (files in order called for) File Name and No.: Input Tapes — File Name and No.: Output Tapes
ØPRS01	
	Computer Operator (Name):

*On Tuesday nights.

Figure 47. 360 Computer Setup—B. Through the courtesy of Crown Zellerbach Corporation.

BAT—105-01/050-00
Date
Company/Division

JOB NO. 532 STEP 5002

JOB NAME: FORD (Rerun) COMPUTER OPERATOR NAME:

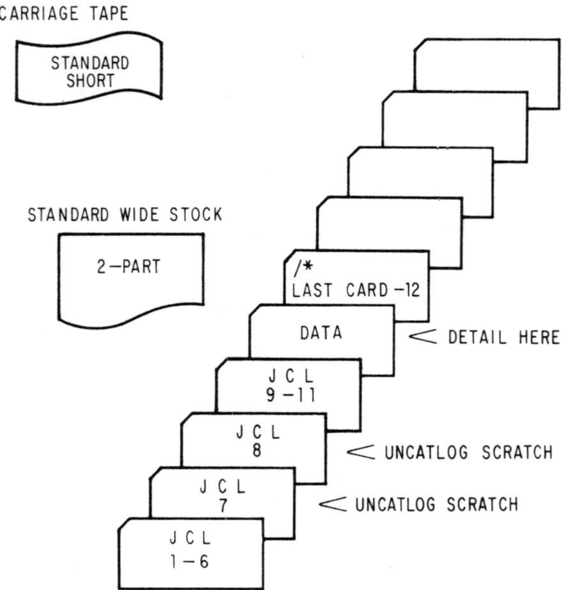

Figure 48. Deck Setup Diagram—B. Through the courtesy of Crown Zellerbach Corporation.

BAT-105-0I/060-00
Date
Company/Division

SAMPLE

SYSTEM NAME: BATHEL Inventory Control System REPORT NAME: Order Report						
REPORT NO. 531-101	FREQUENCY: Weekly					
DISTRIBUTION CLERK NAME: Joan Kelly						
1st COPY:	DECOLLATE	X	BURST		BIND	
DESTINATION: Via Freight—Production Planning OP Converting						
2nd COPY:	DECOLLATE		BURST	X	BIND	
DESTINATION: Production Planning—Bill Nash, Room 297						
3rd COPY:	DECOLLATE		BURST		BIND	
ADDITIONAL INSTRUCTIONS:						

Figure 49. Distribution Instructions. Through the courtesy of Crown Zellerbach Corporation.

BAT-105-0I/070-00
Date
Company/Division

HARDWARE CONFIGURATION (BAT-105-0I/000-00)

The BATHEL Inventory Control System runs on IBM 360/40, uses 94K for its programs, and 5 cylinders of 2314 disk storage. Details of the configuration are:

1. System—Operating System
2. OPRS01—Program Modules
3. DS 0020—Master File
4. DS 0050—Work Areas

The 1403 Printer and the 2540 Reader are the only other peripheral equipment used.

The system running time is about 10 minutes on the above computer and is process bound for about one-half of that time.

SOFTWARE CONFIGURATION (BAT-105-0I/080-00)

The BATHEL Inventory Control System runs under the Operating System Supervisor and uses its catalog and generation data group facilities. The following OS programs are used:

1. IEBGENER
2. SORT-EDIT
3. IEHPROGM

The main program is coded in 18 modules, using Assembly Language, COBOL, and FORTRAN. To reduce the core storage requirements, the main program is overlayed in six segments according to the following structure:

Through the courtesy of Crown Zellerbach Corporation.

BAT-105-0I/080-00
Date
Company/Division

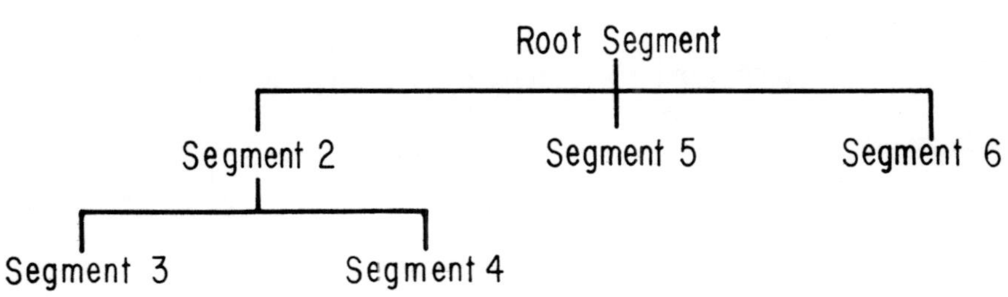

BACKUP FOR EQUIPMENT FAILURE (BAT-105-0I/090-00)

The BATHEL Inventory Control System Master File is copied onto a tape at the beginning of each month. In the event of a disk failure, the tape can be copied back to the disk and the necessary week's rerun.

Four Master File Data Sets are contained on the disk—the latest four weeks. All of this information is available for any rerun.

Through the courtesy of Crown Zellerbach Corporation.

BAT-105-0I/100-00
Date
Company/Division

SAMPL

REFERENCE CHART OF PROGRAMS AND FILES (BAT-105-0I/100-00)

See Book/Section I, General System.

OUTPUT CREATION FLOW TABLE (BAT-105-0I/110-00)

See Book/Section I, General System.

SYSTEM ERROR MESSAGES (BAT-105-0I/120-00)

Self-explanatory.

RESTART PROCEDURE (BAT-105-0I/130-00)

a. Load IEHPROGM and SORT-EDIT from latest BAT tape.
b. Reexecute IEBGENER.

GLOSSARY

access time The amount of time required for a computer to locate and transfer data from a storage device and have it available for processing.

address An identification represented by a name, label, or number for a register, location in storage, or any other data source.

auxiliary memory Storage in addition to the main memory of the computer, for example, magnetic disk, tape, or drum.

ANSCII (American National Standard Code for Information Interchange, X3.4-1968) The standard code that assigns specific bit patterns to each sign, symbol, letter, or number. The coded character consists of 7-bit characters (8 bits including parity check).

batch processing A computing technique in which a set of computer programs are grouped together and processed in a single continuous run for efficient utilization of the computer.

bit A basic symbol, for example, 0, or 1, in the binary system–that is, a unit.

byte A set of 8 bits within a computer word, that is, a unit, usually shorter than a computer word.

central processor unit The main frame of a computer system. It contains the core (main) memory, arithmetic unit and special registers. It is usually abbreviated CPU.

COBOL Common business-oriented language. A commercial (business) data processing language.

compiler An automatic programming routine that processes a source program written in another programming language and produces a machine language routine to accomplish the problem defined by the source program.

CRT display Cathode ray tube display equipment.

delimiter A flag, such as a character, which separates and organizes items of data.

dump To transfer the contents of all or part of a computer memory or storage into another section or type of storage.

dynamic relocation The ability to move programs or data from auxiliary memory into main memory at any convenient location when needed.

EAM Electrical accounting machine.

EBCDIC Extended binary coded decimal interchange code, an 8-bit graphic code used by standard peripheral devices.

file A collection of related records treated as a unit, for example, a sequence of records on magnetic tape terminated by an end-of-file mark or a file gap.

flag An indicator used to qualify an operation for some modification in its processing.

FORTRAN Formula translating system. A procedure-oriented language primarily used for problems expressed in algebraic notation.

format An arrangement of data on a form or storage.

hard copy A visible printout that may be read by the human eye.

index An ordered list of references of the contents of a file or record, together with keys or reference notations for identification or location of the contents. Also, it is a symbol or a numeral used to identify a particular quantity in an array of similar quantities.

interrupt To temporarily stop a process by a special signal from the computer notifying the CPU that some action is required. An interrupt can be generated when a user types a certain command on an input/output device.

label A key consisting of one or more characters, used to identify a body of data (statement or item) in the computer program.

machine language Data represented in a form that is used directly by the computer.

mnemonic code A pseudo-code, represented by symbols or characters that are readily identifiable with information, for example, alphabetic abbreviations.

modem Modulator-Demodulator. A device that modulates and demodulates signals transmitted over communication equipment.

multiprocessing The simultaneous execution of two or more computer programs within a computer system that consists of at least two CPU with a common memory core.

multiprogramming The time-shared use of a single CPU by two or more computer programs.

object program A computer program translated into a language (machine language) that is acceptable to the computer.

OCR Optical character recognition.

offline system Input/output and other peripheral equipment not in direct communication with nor under control of CPU.

online system Input/output devices and all other peripheral equipment under the control of CPU.

operating system Software consisting of executive routines for supervising the execution of computer programs, for example, sequencing, debugging, I/0, compilation, and storage assignment.

overflow The result of a condition in which an operation exceeds the capacity of the register in which the operation is being executed.

overlay A technique of two or more programs or program segments using the same area of memory, though not at the same time. When one routine is completed, another routine replaces it, that is, it is loaded over the first routine.

patch The modification of a routine in a quick-and-dirty manner.

record A collection of related data elements, items, or codes treated as a unit.

source program The computer program written in problem- or procedure-oriented language which is then translated into machine language.

system An organized assembly of related methods or procedures developed according to an integrated scheme to accomplish a specific objective.

time sharing The use of a device for two or more processes by interleaving parts of each process during the same overall time interval.

Index